Richard Brake was born in 1936 and were of the Second World War, a vivid British and German fighter planes over

He was educated at Bristol Grammr enjoyed the sporting activities but, nonetheless, still managed to pass his exams. Upon leaving school he worked for a builders' merchant before being called up for statutory National Service with the Royal Air Force. Most of this time was spent near Tripoli, Libya, and on one occasion he was called out to help fight locusts, which were threatening all the crops on the edge of the Sahara Desert. Again he enjoyed the sporting activities there and, indeed, his love of sport, mainly football, rugby and squash has been lifelong. Following retirement he turned to bowls.

Most of Richard's career was spent in a commercial finance environment and involved negotiations with a wide variety of industries.

He married Joan in 1958 and they had three sons. Their spiritual story began in 1983 following the tragic loss of their eldest son at the age of 21. This led to a spiritual search for the meaning of life and subsequently a quest for knowledge of ancient teachings and wisdom. They visited India several times and spent two months in the USA at an Academy for the study of A Course in Miracles.

With Joan's passing in 2012 Richard gradually developed a gift of channelling which resulted in the publication of his book *Light the Way* in 2014. He follows this with *Realising Spirit Within*, an account of their spiritual journey and experiences, including more channelled and inspirational words from his guides known collectively as Joyful One.

Richard can be contacted via lightthewaybook@btinternet.com

Also by Richard Brake

Light the Way

Realising Spirit Within

Richard Brake

SilverWood

Published in 2018 by SilverWood Books

SilverWood Books Ltd
14 Small Street, Bristol, BS1 1DE, United Kingdom
www.silverwoodbooks.co.uk

Copyright © Richard Brake 2018

The right of Richard Brake to be identified as the author of this work has been asserted in accordance with the Copyright, Designs and Patents Act 1988 Sections 77 and 78.

All rights reserved. No part of this publication may be reproduced, stored in a retrieval system, or transmitted in any form or by any means, electronic, mechanical, photocopying, recording or otherwise, without prior permission of the copyright holder.

The text in this book is written as it was received during channelling sessions. Errors in grammar and punctuation may be present, as all attempts have been made to preserve the original voice.

ISBN 978-1-78132-814-9

British Library Cataloguing in Publication Data
A CIP catalogue record for this book is available from the British Library

Page design and typesetting by SilverWood Books
Printed on responsibly sourced paper

This book is dedicated to the Great Intelligence and Source of life who has inspired all who played a part in creating it.

Contents

Acknowledgements — 9
Foreword — 11
Preface — 15
Introduction — 17
Chapter One — *Journey to Love* — 19
Chapter Two — *Two-Way Communication* — 74
Chapter Three — *On the Pathway* — 108
Chapter Four — *Ready to Serve* — 146
Chapter Five — *Creation and Science* — 163
Chapter Six — *Inner Realms* — 187
Chapter Seven — *Experiencing Sai Baba* — 197
Chapter Eight — *Meditation* — 211
Chapter Nine — *Oneness* — 226
Chapter Ten — *Realising Spirit Within* — 243
Epilogue — 275

Acknowledgements

I acknowledge with love and gratitude my friends in spirit known as Joyful One together with those higher beings who, through inspiration and with channelling, brought words into my mind to form the teachings in this book.

A special mention is given to Jan Passmore who has assisted me throughout by providing inspiration and advice during the production of *Realising Spirit Within* as well as editing the content.

My grateful thanks go to Thelma Dawber for writing the foreword to the book and who, together with other members of spiritual circles I attend, provided the setting and opportunities for many of the teachings.

Many thanks also to John Ward for giving me permission to use the first verse of his song 'Dear Soul' on the cover of this book.

Finally, thank you to all who have in any way helped and encouraged me to present this book.

Foreword

It seems only five minutes and not thirty-five years since Joan, Richard and I met at Clevedon Spiritualist Church one Sunday afternoon. It felt as though we already knew each other and Joan and I discovered that we shared the same sense of humour.

Although I have always followed the path of Spiritualism, Joan and Richard subsequently became devotees of Sai Baba in India. They took groups to Puttaparthi and held many meetings in this country. Their generosity and love was always freely given.

My friendship with them has stood the test of time, and continues, with Richard and I now meeting weekly to speak and record the words we are given from spirit. At one such meeting I received the following channelling which I wish to share here. The words compare the human condition to a river of life with all its twists and turns; just as the river finally merges with the sea so humanity conjoins itself with the God force.

I feel sure you will enjoy reading, and passing on to others, the wisdom in this book.

Thelma Dawber

> We would like to compare this human life to a river of life. As a river begins at the top of a mountain, equivalent to when you were first born, the clouds come over and drip their water onto the mountains. The mountains squeeze the water down through the valleys, over the rocks, forging a deep crevasse because the rivers are narrow. Their force and power represent the youth of humanity.
>
> As the gradient becomes less, and the human becomes older, there is a levelling out of the river. It becomes full of nourishment,

for the life which is in it reflects the help you give to other people. The great power which comes down with the rivers is, of course, that power from the Creator which leads the river to the ocean and there is much life drawn to the river. Creatures, plants, trees, everything in that river depends upon this river of life, particularly mankind who will put upon it his boats and make use of it to catch the fish which have swum up the river; curious, or to lay their eggs.

This river of life feeds all that it touches and, gradually, it spreads itself out as all the other rivers have joined it. The streams have become rivers and the rivers have become one big river which flows into the sea. On the plain it is flat; the river floods the plains and the goodness, which has been brought down by the river, is like mankind spreading even further that which it has within it.

The river, like mankind, flows to the sea, the sea being the latter part of life: a joining of the waters, a true spirituality for mankind as he travels further on his spiritual way to be encompassed by the ocean of the Godhead, that vast love that is never-ending which holds all in its thrall, the power of which is inimitable. This may seem a strange analogy but we take you to the thought that this power has been with you all your lives, that energy as described with the river, that understanding and knowledge has come with you throughout your lives.

There is no going back; you cannot go up the river again, you cannot go back to your childhood except, of course, in the mind. You have conjoined yourself with the God force and followed your own pathway. Although there have been deviations on the way they have been necessary for you to learn a little more of the personalities of the people with whom you have mixed, those who you have felt drawn to and those you have felt the need to walk away from.

That inherent knowledge within you has helped you every step of that river's journey. There has been no faltering; you have been true to yourselves and to the God within you and all along your pathway you have had the help of spirit, the inspiration which has been within you and has pushed you sometimes to walk on the right path, to say the right thing, to instantly, instinctively, know what is right and what is wrong.

Preface

In my book *Light the Way* I explained how my contact with spirit – or should I say their contact with me – began after my wife, Joan, left her physical body in 2012 and we began an exchange of letters. I subsequently started to receive and channel spiritual teachings and advice, followed by teachings on a direct basis. These were from my guides in spirit who had given their collective name as Joyful One. Communication continues to this day.

Joan and I had many spiritual adventures, both here and in India. Now, I have been inspired by Joyful One to share some of them with you in the first chapter of this book. The remaining chapters are devoted to direct communication; teachings received from spirit during personal meditation and in circles when like-minded friends were present. I have also included talks given on my travels when requested to channel by those present.

Again, the teachings cover a wide range of topics and separating them into book form has not been easy, especially when several subjects overlap. The overriding message stresses the importance of becoming aware of one's inner self, that part of the heart area where one can feel the Christ Spirit.

Most people, leading a busy life, do not make sufficient time for contemplation and relaxation of the mind, but when we succeed clear thinking and inspiration often follow. This happened to me one day when meditating; only three words came into my mind and I instantly knew these would form the book title. Once the order of the chapters had been established this led naturally to the zenith of the teachings, *Realising Spirit Within*.

It is a privilege to have been given the opportunity to compile this second book and, as you read, I wish you love, enjoyment and success on your inward journey.

Introduction

My whole body seems to be tingling as I await contact – words and feelings from spirit. My fingers are warm; my heart feels alive expanding the glorious feeling within. As this feeling grows it takes over the top half of my body, goes down the arms, meeting the hands. My head and shoulders, too, are filled with peace: stillness.

The tingling has stopped and been replaced with a feeling of Oneness and expansion throughout the rest of my body. As I sit here in bliss, receiving and sending out, it feels as though my body is being recharged and, yet, it is sending out love and healing which is making a circle of energy. The body is filled with love and healing and is reaching out with hands held high and the feeling now is of connection, Oneness, with the air around and with those from spirit and all life.

Yes, the circuit is complete and I rest in the knowledge that energy is coming in and going out; that energy of love and healing. It is coming from All That Is and is going to All That Is and, particularly, to the people on earth who are in such need at this time.

So, as I continue to be a transformer I cannot help but feel the energy within every cell of my body. I now have a feeling of timelessness; hey, I feel ageless as I am absorbed into the Oneness of the Great Spirit. I stay here in this state for as long as I can, but I know that as I am in this world I will soon go about my business for the day. I know that, within, I have received direct from spirit the energy, the confidence, the will, to be of service in this life.

Chapter One

Journey to Love

I recollect that my earliest religious memories are from junior school in the 1940s. The emphasis was firmly on the Christian faith and each morning at assembly we dutifully sang hymns and said prayers. From this background, I became a choirboy at the local church when about ten years old.

Two years later my family moved to a different area of Bristol. I continued to sing in a church choir and, eventually, was confirmed into the Church of England. In my late teens I became a server, assisting the priest at Holy Communion, but in spite of this I could not claim any special attachment to the Church. Even later, I still did not hold any strong religious beliefs.

In retrospect, becoming a choirboy and then a server had seemed right at the time and appeared to be an automatic choice, rather than a reasoned one. However, my belief now is that there is no such thing as coincidence, so I wonder…

Many years later, having married Joan and together brought up three boys, any thoughts of religion had long drifted away. Then, as a bolt from the blue, came the tragic death of our eldest son, Duncan, in 1983. The circumstances of his death, when he committed suicide, left our family devastated and numb. Our second son, Peter, was already working on the south coast of England and Edward, our youngest son, still lived at home. Joan and I were both extremely worried about him as he was only sixteen years old and had been particularly close to Duncan.

One evening, shortly afterwards, when we had both retired to bed, Joan prayed, 'if there is a God, please let Duncan look after Edward.' A little later she heard the front door open and, as our room faced the top of the stairs with the door always open, Joan saw Edward coming upstairs with, she assumed, a friend wearing what looked like a bright crash helmet. As Edward turned at the top of the stairs to go into his bedroom at the end of the landing the 'friend' passed straight through Edward and into the bedroom immediately on the left, Duncan's room! Joan said in that moment she knew her prayer had been answered. Unfortunately, I had fallen asleep and missed this phenomenon so was stunned when Joan related this incredible experience. Yet, I believed it to be true.

Some three years later a small book, called *The Book of Light*, came into our hands at a spiritualist church in Portsmouth. Upon opening it, our eyes were immediately drawn to the illustration inside the front cover which depicted a head surrounded by an illuminated, bright aura. Amazingly, it bore an uncanny resemblance to what Joan had seen a few years before and taken to be a crash helmet.

Our lives were on hold following Duncan's death. Everything seemed to stop at that moment, yet appeared to continue as normal for everyone else.

All my thoughts and attitudes changed from this time, for it was a complete shock to my system, especially as Duncan took his own life in such dramatic circumstances. We were unaware of the drug problem until after his death. He was twenty-one years old and had left home on and off over a number of years, but he had seemed relatively settled in London when, only a few weeks before, we spent the day together.

Initially, Joan and I were completely distraught, but so immensely grateful to our friends and relations for their overwhelming support. Fortunately, the tragedy brought us closer as a family and we gradually dealt with the aftermath and the painful process of rebuilding our lives.

Soon after returning to work, when I was alone in the office, the cleaning lady who had heard about our loss explained that her six-year-old daughter had been killed in London a few years earlier on a pedestrian crossing. She said that books on the afterlife had helped her and she lent me one by Doris Stokes, a well-known clairvoyant at the time. I had no religious beliefs then and was sceptical about life after death. However, I read the book and was intrigued with stories of loved ones making contact from the other side through Doris. As time went on I read another one of her books and eighteen months later Joan announced that she was going to attend the local spiritualist church. She was surprised when I responded by saying that we would go together.

For those unfamiliar with Spiritualism, a registered religion and way of life, a divine service is held with prayers, hymns, a reading and an address. It differs from orthodox services in that readings are taken from any spiritual philosophical book and, during the latter part of the service, the medium demonstrates the continuance of life after death by relaying words and visions received from the spirit world. A good medium can describe the person now in spirit, often temporarily feeling pain in the body as he or she explains how the passing occurred. The messages are sometimes humorous, with names occasionally offered together with words of advice, where appropriate, and sometimes the information given is known only to the recipient. In proving the continuance of life, much comfort is brought to those who are grieving and searching spiritually. A very warm welcome is given and new people are quickly put at ease by the friendliness and love they receive.

So, the day came when we went to our first spiritualist service. I was very nervous but fascinated by the medium talking about spiritual healing in his address. After the next hymn, he gave messages to a few people and, as time was running out, the chairperson said there was only time for one short message. I couldn't believe it as the medium came to me saying he wanted to talk to 'the man with a moustache wearing a blazer'. I looked around the room but I was the only one who fitted the description. I have always remembered it because it was on 2 February, my mother's birthday; she had passed to spirit eight years previously. The medium said he had my mother with him and she was calling me 'me duck' an endearment which she had often used when alive. She said she was so sorry for what we had been through recently and gave us both her love.

Joan and I continued to attend spiritualist services on a regular basis and received several messages, including contact from Duncan, which meant so much. However, there was one communication which finally convinced me, without a shadow of doubt, that there is life after death. As the medium came to me he started coughing, loudly and distinctively, and eventually succeeded in spluttering the name George Hann… cough…ah (George Hannah). George had been a friend of the family when I was a young boy and I affectionately called him Uncle George. He smoked incessantly and had the most unique cough which seemed to go on for minutes rather than seconds. Well, the medium coughed in exactly the same way as my uncle had done all those years ago.

A small thing you might think, but to hear his most unusual cough replicated in this way was an undeniable truth.

Within weeks of attending our first spiritualist church service, Joan and I were invited to join a development circle. In truth we were not sufficiently experienced to attend, so the first meeting was naturally a little uncomfortable for us. We were asked to go into the silence (meditation) for some time and then relate our experiences, but we did not see or feel anything.

The following weekend we attended the annual conference of 41 Club, of which I was a member. On the way into Blackpool we noticed a spiritualist church and decided to go on Sunday afternoon after the conference, which finished at lunch time.

We were surprised to receive a message and quite amazed at the content, being told that we had just joined a circle and that it wouldn't last. We were informed that we would soon hear that it had come to an end. Sure enough, upon returning home we found a letter confirming that the circle had, indeed, finished. Naively, we questioned how the medium would be able to give us a message about things happening at home when we were 300 miles away. Of course, we later realised that distance and time is no barrier to those in spirit relaying messages through a medium.

In time, Joan and I became more involved as members of the local spiritualist church, holding positions on the committee. It had occurred to us that there was never sufficient time for discussion of spiritual matters after church services, so we decided to start a weekly discussion group at our home where various spiritual topics could be raised and explored.

Additionally, we started monthly meetings, also at our home, inviting speakers to give a talk on their specialised subject. These included spiritual healing, numerology, astrology, theosophy, shiatsu, trance mediumship, raja yoga, crystal energy and Atlantis. This, too, provided a good source for debate at our weekly meetings.

Shortly after starting the discussion group we were invited to join two circles, one development and the other a twelve-week teaching one. Fortunately, the circles did not conflict but, rather, each enhanced the other. This time we felt very comfortable with both circles and learned a great deal about spiritual healing, mediumship and spiritual philosophy.

We continued to receive many messages at church from family and friends who had passed to spirit, including Duncan who presented himself through the medium as a happy young man again. These communications were incredibly accurate, and in some cases required investigation into the past to confirm the information given from the platform.

I obviously cannot recall all the messages received in church and circle, but remember they were nearly always positive and encouraging. However, one memorable message was given to me in September 1987 when the medium said she saw a new, bright-red car being delivered to me. At the time, I was fortunate enough to drive a company car, a Ford or Vauxhall, which was changed every three years. It so happened that a change of car was imminent with the choice of colour left to me. I didn't believe in making messages fit so I ordered my favourite colour, blue, and a new Vauxhall Astra was delivered to me soon afterwards.

Imagine my surprise when three months later, while attending my company's annual conference, I received an award for the best profit figures in my region. The prize was a new BMW company car, to be delivered the following week. I was in the office when one of the secretaries answered the telephone and called over to me to say that the new car would be delivered the next day. I asked her to enquire what colour it was and I am sure you know what is coming. Yes, I couldn't believe it when she said it was red!

Joan and I were practising spiritual healers when we became acquainted with a lady who was to be part of our lives for several months.

We had met in church when a medium described her as being very spiritual. Whilst in our presence she was nearly always dressed in white and spent most of the time meditating, whether she was travelling in the car with us or when relaxing in our home. We accepted her into our lives and spent a lot of time with her, both at our home and on visits to churches and workshops during our search for spiritual knowledge. She gave us the impression of being from the angelic realms, but in an earthly body.

Following many discussions with this lady we had grown to respect and love her, and we reached the conclusion that, together, we would like to open a healing sanctuary in southern Spain. She made arrangements for us to stay in new villas being offered for sale or time-share. To set up a sanctuary in Spain would have entailed leaving my job and selling our home to raise the finance needed. I even saw a solicitor to discuss the ramifications of setting up such a venture.

We visited Spain three times and, at this stage, were close to putting our house up for sale. However, the day inevitably came when we discovered that this lady was using us. Although she gave the impression of being very spiritual we found out that she was not who she purported to be. We had been taken in by what she said and portrayed.

When the truth came out we were both shocked and dismayed. We went to see her to call an end to the project and our association with her. Fortunately, we had not taken any drastic decision about my resignation at work and had not yet put our house up for sale.

Shortly after this we received a message from spirit confirming that we had made the right decision and that the person involved was delusional. Looking back, one can see how this association developed in our early, impressionable, searching days but it was a warning that all may not always be as it seems and we put it down to experience.

The incident made us both stronger and did not affect our faith in God but, rather, gave us confidence to go forward in our drive for spiritual knowledge and made us more aware of people who want to use others for their own aims. So, without being too suspicious about people who came into our lives after this, we did not allow ourselves to be taken in again as we moved forward in life, ready and more equipped for what lay ahead.

My grandfather, who passed to spirit when I was twelve, often gave me spiritual guidance in the form of messages from the platform. He was always presented as strong and strict as he had been in the body.

One day, after church, we were invited back to the home of a friend, Billy Thomas. Billy was a Minister of the Spiritualist Church and he brought with him a visiting medium from Northampton who had the gift of transfiguration. When this occurs a medium's face can take on the look, or image, of someone who has passed to spirit. After a little while Billy asked the medium if he had anyone from spirit with him. Joan and I were intrigued and, I have to say, a little amused, as the medium's face began to distort and go into strange contortions. Incredibly, as it gradually settled down it became the easily identifiable face of my late grandfather, which was a huge surprise. It seemed so appropriate as I had received regular supportive and helpful messages from him.

A little later the medium's face once more started to distort, again to the silent amusement of Joan and I. No disrespect was intended but we just couldn't stop ourselves. As the medium's face settled, Billy was quite overcome to see his grandmother's face revealed. Billy had, in his younger days, been in a physical circle and often regaled us with stories of his remarkable experiences, when spirit visitors sometimes materialised into the look and shape of their previous earthly bodies. Sometimes they were friends, relations, or the guide of one of the sitters. Once or twice Billy had actually been invited to touch the figure, which had been formed out of ectoplasm emitting from the bodies of the physical medium and sitters.

In 1989 Billy, together with some medium friends, asked us if we would be willing to hold a physical circle in our home, to which we agreed. However, after a year, and before any physical phenomena occurred, Joan and I left the circle as by that time we were increasingly involved in the Sathya Sai Baba Organisation. The circle subsequently moved its location to Bristol and became known as the Omega Circle.

Fast forward over twenty years… The Omega Circle is still here providing love and help to those people who are occasionally invited as guests. The make-up of the circle has changed with a few members leaving, including Billy who passed to spirit several years ago, and new members joining. Andrew Western is now the physical trance medium, having developed the gift of transfiguration. In circle the faces of loved ones, guides and well-known people who have passed to spirit appear on Andrew's face, without the need for the contortions that Joan and I had seen previously at Billy's house.

One evening, soon after Joan left her earthly body, I was fortunate to be invited to the Omega Circle as a guest. Andrew's first guide was complimentary to me as he made a point of saying I was one of the founder members, together with Joan, of the circle all those years before: a fact unknown to one or two of the current sitters. After bringing through my Chinese healing guide, Andrew's face transfigured into the shape of Joan's face and I was invited to sit next to him. Joan spoke in a whisper, through Andrew to me, and, amazingly, we conversed for a few minutes.

Joan confirmed that it was she who, in the middle of the night, had turned on my hi-fi a few months after her transition. This had woken me up and it was playing one of our favourite songs, 'Dear Soul', written by John Ward and sung by Renu Gidoomal, two of our dearest friends. The incident was remarkable as the hi-fi had been turned off before I went to bed and it was a hard-disk-type to which all the data from my CDs had been transferred. This was all the more astounding because not only had the machine to be switched on but it was also necessary to select one song from all the albums now on the hard disk. Joan also admitted that she had fused all the lights in the house when I switched on a wall light in the lounge one evening. There was a bang and all the other lights went out. I guessed it was her, hence my question at the Omega Circle.

Three years later, on 31 May 2015, I was fortunate to be present at a public demonstration given by the Circle at Clevedon Spiritualist Church. Andrew Western was again the physical trance medium and the sitters, who selflessly give power to and protect the medium, were virtually the same as before.

Imagine my surprise when Billy Thomas came through. He spoke to me with the same strong Welsh accent and very outgoing personality he had portrayed during his life. I have included here a transcript of this part of the meeting (which had been recorded) to demonstrate the accuracy and quality of Andrew's mediumship. Fred is the leader of the Circle.

> BILLY *Hello Richard.*
> RICHARD Hello.
> BILLY *Joan's fine, by the way.*
> RICHARD Thank you.
> BILLY *I bet your ears are better now because she used to give you a little bit of that, didn't she? (Billy opened and closed his hand quickly by his mouth).*
> RICHARD You know too much!
> BILLY *I was the one – and I think Frederick will understand this – I was the one who got this medium going in the circle.*
> FRED That's right.
> BILLY (Animatedly). *I was in the circle. I was the one…you remember Jean and Marian, lovely people…I was the one that started all this. It was to be physical. I remember when it started. We were down Richard and Joan's house in the room with the trumpet, trying to get the b***** to move, but it didn't work.*

This exchange was so true, meaningful and relevant to me in view of our past friendship.

In 1988, as our search deepened, various spiritual books came into our hands, one being about a teacher called Sai Baba who lived on an ashram in southern India and Joan had a dream about Him.

Further mention of Sai Baba came on two occasions at church services. Then, coincidentally, no less than four consecutive speakers at our monthly discussion group meetings spent the last ten minutes or so of their presentations speaking about Him, although not the intended subject of their lectures.

Subsequently, we visited the Ramala Centre in Glastonbury run by Ann and David Jevons. We had read their books *The Revelation of Ramala*, *The Wisdom of Ramala*, and *The Vision of Ramala*. These contained channelled spiritual teachings received from a higher plane of consciousness, through a source named Ramala. David and Ann had been told several years earlier that they would work together to ground a spiritual point of consciousness on earth. From early beginnings they moved to Chalice Hill House, which became known as the Ramala Centre, a retreat for meditation, channelling, counselling, seminars and workshops.

During our visit we came across further Sai Baba books, including *Man of Miracles* by Howard Murphet, *The Holy Man and the Psychiatrist* by Dr Sam Sandweiss and *The Embodiment of Love* by Peggy Mason and Ron Laing.

Next, we discovered that Sai Baba group meetings were held in Bath and in other parts of southern England. They varied from devotional meetings, including Sai Baba's teachings, seminars with guest speakers outlining their experiences, questions and answers etc. We began attending, and at one meeting were so fortunate to hear a talk given by Peggy and Ron as it was one of their last, prior to retirement. They were a very popular and knowledgeable couple and related some of their many experiences.

Little did we realise that, gradually, we were being drawn more and more towards India.

On another occasion we attended a raja yoga meditation in Bristol. Raja yoga is known as the royal path to unity with mind, body and spirit by the control and mastery of the mind and emotions, leading to the mind being connected to God, the source of spiritual power. Whilst there we met a lady who told us of a tape recording on which the speaker had given an account of his experiences with Sai Baba. She was thinking of visiting Sai Baba and kindly showed us a copy of Peggy Mason's magazine containing details of arranged group visits to the ashram in Puttaparthi. Upon our leaving, she promised to send the magazine which we promptly received. Incidentally, the recording later proved to be one of our tapes as all our monthly meetings were recorded!

We were now feeling the call to visit India and before long we were on our way. Our group leaders were Aimé and Sandra Levy, with whom we formed a lasting friendship.

It is quite astonishing how so-called coincidences like this happen. When the pupil is ready the master appears.

Throughout the book I have used capital letters when referring to Sai Baba. He was, and still is, widely regarded as an Avatar (incarnation of God) and I, too, regard Him as such based on my experiences in His presence, together with an inner knowing. His devotees regarded Him as God and He proved His omnipresence, omnipotence and omniscience on countless occasions and often said:

> *'I am you; you are Me.'*
> *'You are the waves; I am the ocean.'*
> *'Know this and be free; be divine.'*

When Joan and I first heard of Sai Baba we remarked that His teachings and miracles strikingly resembled those of Jesus. It therefore seemed a natural progression in our search to visit India and investigate for ourselves.

The day finally came, in late January 1990, for our first visit to India to see the holy man and Avatar, Sai Baba. One month before the visit Joan and I, together with the other members of the party, attended a group meeting with our leaders, Aimé and Sandra, so we could all become better acquainted. It was particularly necessary for first time visitors to learn the travel and hotel details, information for the pilgrimage regarding dress, food, sleeping arrangements, rules of the ashram and the typical daily routine. I will paint a fuller picture of life on the ashram when recounting some of our later visits.

After a nine-hour flight to Bombay, now called Mumbai, we made our way from the international airport to the domestic airport, ready for our internal flight to Bangalore. Nothing had quite prepared us for the sight of a shanty town as we approached the domestic airport. The large area of huts, sometimes with tin roofs, many others without any living accommodation, and all with no sign of any material goods, contrasted so vividly with the more affluent areas of the city.

At the airport we were surrounded by young and old people from the shanty town, some wanting to carry our cases hoping for a tip: most of the others begging for money. Apparently, some of the beggars even maimed themselves, or their children, to appeal to people's generosity. We eventually reached the departure lounge and waited a few hours for our connected flight to Bangalore. Upon arrival we were ushered into taxis and taken to two separate hotels, just in time for breakfast.

We heard that Sai Baba was at His ashram, called Brindavan, just outside Bangalore at a village called Whitefield. After recovering from our flights, we were ready to visit the ashram in the early evening. Two old coaches arrived and took us across town to Whitefield, where we arrived in plenty of time for darshan and joined the waiting queue of people. Men and women were placed in separate areas and we all joined rows awaiting the customary drawing of numbered tokens from a bag, to determine in which order the rows entered the darshan area. We sat on the floor and were allowed to take cushions with us, but those who could not sit on the floor were allocated chairs on the side, although this usually meant being further away from Sai Baba when He came among us to give His darshan (blessing on all).

There was a sudden hush and all eyes turned towards His house. Sai Baba entered the sand-covered courtyard and walked gracefully towards the thousands of people awaiting His presence. Our group members all had different experiences of Him, varying from feeling nothing, to someone seeing the colour of His aura as gold and filling the area of the whole ashram. (An aura is the electro-magnetic field that surrounds the human body and all living beings. Each aura is unique, as are its array of colours, often seen by people with that gift. The variety and strength of the colours reflect one's state of being, including health, spiritual progress, attitude, and love for others).

We had our own individual darshan as Sai Baba walked among us, collecting letters and stopping now and then to say a few words to people who had their hands raised in prayer. Most visitors, or devotees, wrote at least one letter to Sai Baba, requesting help for themselves or others and often for an interview. It was well-known that He read all the letters that He collected and it was considered a welcome and grace for Sai Baba to take one's own letter. As He passed our group of men He asked our leader, 'How many?' the question which we had been told often led to an interview. After the reply, 'Ninety' Sai Baba said, 'too many' and moved on. One or two other groups were invited for interview and the remainder of us, who were sitting on the floor, were just grateful to be in His presence.

Sai Baba stayed in Bangalore for a few more days and then went to Madras, now called Chennai. Some of our group decided to follow Him, the rest of us went to Puttaparthi, the site of Sai Baba's main ashram and residence in southern India. The ashram is called Prasanthi Nilayam, meaning abode of highest peace, and is situated over one hundred miles north of Bangalore. Even though Sai Baba was in Madras, there was a special warmth in the ashram and it felt as though He was present. We attended bhajans (devotional songs of praise to God) which were sung morning and evening and acclimatised ourselves to a simple way of life for the next seven days.

In addition to the Sai Centres at Channai and Mumbai there are also centres at Whitefield, already mentioned, and at Kodaikanal, a hill station in southern India near Madurai. Kodaikanal was used by Sai Baba and His devotees when the summer temperature became too hot.

News reached us that Sai Baba would be returning to Whitefield, so we decided to make our way back to Bangalore and stay in the same hotels as before. We arrived in the evening and were all up very early the next morning to await the arrival of coaches to take us to the ashram. We waited and waited, with telephone calls made to the coach company, and were repeatedly told, 'the coaches are coming'. They eventually arrived two hours late and we thought we had missed morning darshan, but Sai Baba came out much later than usual as though He had been awaiting us, for as soon as we were seated He came across the courtyard. It was the same routine as last time and the same question, 'How many?' was greeted by the same answer, 'ninety'. Again, Sai Baba said, 'Too many'.

Before we came to India we had expected to split into three groups of thirty each but, due to some devotees going to Madras, we hadn't had the opportunity to separate under three leaders. After speaking to us Sai Baba moved along the line and asked another English devotee, 'How many?' and the reply was, 'nine' which received the wonderful response of, 'go', meaning an interview.

We later held a group meeting and decided that it was too late in the pilgrimage to split into three. Those who desperately needed an interview, for reasons such as serious illness, were asked to see our leaders after the meeting to form a smaller group in the hope of an interview. The next day when Sai Baba came for darshan He selected this group for interview and the rest of us were delighted for them.

This was the first of our many visits to Sai Baba which were to be full of many remarkable incidents.

The following year, January 1991, we were once more on our way to see Sai Baba. On this occasion He was at Whitefield and our leaders, Aimé and Sandra, had already separated us into three groups. We were again fortunate to have the wonderful experience of darshan, morning and evening, when Sai Baba walked among us talking to people, taking letters and sometimes materialising vibhuti (holy ash) by a swirl of His hand, letting it come through His fingers into the palm of an expectant devotee.

Vibhuti, used during Hindu rituals, is normally made from dried burnt wood. Its benefits are said to increase positive energy, regulate the chakras (invisible energy centres in the body) and reminds us of the impermanence of life, thereby decreasing our worldly desires and increasing our compassion for others. It has been said that ash is ash forever and, in this state, it reminds us of our true nature which is unchanging.

> Vibhuti is a constant reminder of the evanescence of the body which, ultimately, is reduced in cremation to a potful of ash.
>
> *(Sai Baba)*

Vibhuti also appears seemingly out of nowhere on photographs of Sai Baba, even on the glass frames. I have seen a huge amount of vibhuti on photographs at houses in Kuala Lumpur, and London as well as locally, on a photograph at a friend's house.

One morning at darshan we noticed Sai Baba was speaking to our leader and, almost before we realised it, Aimé was on his feet as he had been given the magic word 'go' for interview. It was indescribable to be in Sai Baba's presence in the small interview room. We were sitting on the floor, men on the left and ladies on the right, when He stood up and materialised vibhuti for the ladies; somehow there was sufficient for them all. He spoke to us as a group, and individually to a few, but some were so overcome they could not reply.

Our party included a young man in a wheelchair and an older man having difficulty walking, so when Sai Baba materialised gold rings for them they were very emotional. Baba had stated publicly that He gave people trinkets and trash until they were ready for what He had come to give them:

> You have come to get from Me tinsel and trash, petty cures and promotions, worldly joys and comforts. Very few of you desire to get from Me the thing I have come to give you, namely, liberation itself.
> *(Sai Baba)*

After speaking again, He sang, in English, a bhajan He had written. The following opening lines express His purpose and the tenet of His teachings:

> *Love is my form, truth is my breath, bliss is my food*
> *My life is my message, expansion is my life*
> *No reason for love, no season for love*
> *No birth, no death...*

It was sung with such feeling and love that some were reduced to tears; others, like me, were spellbound. At the same time, I was experiencing His love filling not only my heart area but my whole body. When the interview was over Baba handed everyone a few packets of vibhuti, which had been made in the traditional way, but had been blessed by Him. The packets had previously been filled by devotees as an act of service. We returned across the courtyard in total bliss, having been in very close contact with this holy teacher.

After this first interview life was never quite the same again. To have been able to sit close to this great teacher who used to say, 'I am God and you are God, the only difference is that I know it and you don't', was such a blessing. Having been in the same room as Him, feeling His unconditional love, was like being flooded with His energy and it stayed with me wherever I went. My whole body seemed to be permanently uplifted and any hardship or problem melted away.

Over the rest of the decade Joan and I were very fortunate to receive several more interviews and had wonderful experiences in His presence: memories which still live with me today.

We made our third visit to India in October 1991 and this time Joan and I were leaders of one group, within the overall direction of Aimé and Sandra.

The full three weeks were spent at Sai Baba's main ashram at Puttaparthi and we soon settled into life there. Joan and I considered ourselves very fortunate to be allocated a totally empty one-roomed flat. Some visitors were directed to what was aptly known as a 'shed', where the accommodation was very basic and noisy. It was usual to hire a camp bed and buy a cheap mattress; that was it. The living conditions on the ashram were austere.

Traditional, hotly spiced, food could be purchased in the main canteen, but at busy periods on the ashram a canteen catering for Western tastes was opened. Everyone took turns at the menial tasks. The cooking was undertaken by a large group of devotees from Italy, who always visited around this time of year, carrying out these duties as service.

A normal day started at five o'clock in the morning, with Omkar in the mandir (temple), when twenty-one OMs were chanted, the OM being the primeval sound. Sai Baba described it as the verbal symbol of God; the only sound, every other sound arising from it. He also said that when chanting OM, we are calling God. As there were many thousands at the ashram every day, it was a rare privilege to be present in the temple, even once, as it held only a few hundred people. I remember well the occasion when the energy within my body, as the OMs were chanted, was so strong that it equalled the sound levels produced in the temple which, in themselves, were deafening. A truly, once in a lifetime, amazing experience.

This was followed by a procession of singers, which gradually wound its way from the temple to the main gate, and anyone who wished to join in could do so. This was known as Nagar Sankirtan (singing holy songs in your neighbourhood).

> When you participate in the early hours of the day your heart will be brimming with bliss. It is not merely kirtan (singing) it is sankirtan (singing together wholeheartedly) to experience and

share your joy with one and all. Sing His glory full-throated and make everyone drink the nectar of the Divine name. In fact, the motive of all your endeavours should be expansion of heart and joy for all. Only then will you be worthy of the title of human being. Then only is your life as a human being worthwhile. *(Sai Baba)*

After this it was time to queue in lines ready for darshan. As I previously mentioned, numbered tokens were selected by the first person in each line, which determined the order in which everyone entered. The first line would, therefore, be nearest to Sai Baba when He came out for darshan. During the wait, which could be up to a couple of hours, devotees usually spent the time meditating.

Shortly before darshan commenced, students from His schools and university came into their allocated areas and they, too, were ready for Him to move between them talking to some, taking letters, etc. as He completed darshan. Then bhajans were sung in the temple and outside, where many people remained after darshan as Sai Baba was present during the singing.

Then, time for breakfast followed by group meetings or lectures given by knowledgeable devotees who lived permanently on the ashram. On certain days, the group visited places of interest in Puttaparthi, including Sai Baba's birthplace, the Meditation tree, the compound of His elephant Sai Gita (since replaced by Sathya Gita), and also the Wish-fulfilling tree where the young Sai Baba could pick any variety of fruit, just by materialising it!

Additionally, there was the Planetarium, now called the Space Theatre, and the Hill View Stadium which hosted the annual sports day, as well as Sai Baba's birthday celebrations. The Eternal Heritage Museum promotes one of Baba's cardinal teachings which is the unity of all religions. It also highlights the main precepts of each religion and the lives and teachings of great saints and spiritual masters.

The Super Specialty Hospital, on the outskirts of Puttaparthi, has been described as a magnificent temple of healing, with its inspiring architecture imparting an aura of divinity and peace to all who enter. It was designed by Professor Keith Critchlow and Jonathan Allen from London. There is a huge dome at the entrance, creating a large space within; each time we took a group to visit I was always overcome with emotion standing there. I seemed to be at one with everything and everyone.

It was always such a pleasure to visit and to be greeted with smiling faces. Everything gleamed with cleanliness and from the light shining through the specially designed windows.

The hospital was established by Sai Baba in 1991 after He had announced twelve months earlier that it would be designed and built within a year; a miracle. Sai Baba laid down four guiding principles:

Universal Healthcare – Healthcare should be available to all, irrespective of caste, religion, nationality, or financial status.
De-commercialised Healthcare – Healthcare should be delivered free of charge.
Human Values in Healthcare – Healthcare should be administered with love.
Spiritualisation of Healthcare – The aim should be to heal the patient in body, mind and spirit, not merely to cure disease.

We were so blessed to receive two group interviews on this visit to the ashram. During one of them I suddenly found myself standing up requesting a private interview. This was most out of character for me as in no way could I be described as an extrovert. Baba replied, 'Yes', and I then said, 'my wife, too?' He answered, 'Yes, your wife is your life, your other half.' Joan and I already felt that we had known each other in previous lives and could be twin souls.

The private interview was amazing. Being in the inner room with Swami (the name He liked to be addressed by) felt dreamlike. He was so loving; He told us about Duncan and explained in detail his state of mind and reasons for taking his life. He also spoke of other matters, which were known only to us, including our relationship and that we argued sometimes, but now all was good and He was very happy. He encouraged us with the work we were doing and we were both filled with an incredible feeling of bliss.

We returned home full of vigour and enthusiasm to continue the work Sai Baba was obviously giving us to do, by providing a platform for people to learn of Him and His teachings and holding regular meetings in our area. Sai Baba open days and national weekends would follow.

Our next pilgrimage to Sai Baba was in 1992, for the Christmas celebrations.

Our party reached Mumbai in the middle of the night, and spent a few hours resting in a hotel before making our way to the domestic airport. Little did we know that, shortly after we had left the hotel, riots had begun in Mumbai but, fortunately, the rioters had not reached the airport and our plane to Bangalore took off without incident. We heard later that the riots started because Hindu extremists had destroyed the famous Ayodhya Muslim Mosque during the night and the violence quickly spread to many parts of India, including Bangalore.

We usually stayed for a day or two in Bangalore before travelling to Prasanthi Nilayam but, for some extraordinary reason, advance arrangements had been made for us to stay several miles outside the city. We arrived safely, still unaware of the riots, but when we heard that they had spread to Bangalore we stayed at the hotel until it was safe to travel by road to the ashram. Luckily, we had an incident-free journey and felt we had been protected as we did not see any sign of trouble on the way.

Christmas, spent in the ashram, was unforgettable. It confirmed our belief that this was, indeed, the way to celebrate it, without the commercialism prevalent in the Western world. All visitors were given the opportunity to join a choir and we spent many happy hours rehearsing the 'Hallelujah Chorus' from *Messiah* and several English devotional songs, including carols. On Christmas Eve we performed in front of Sai Baba and all the other devotees. He seemed very pleased and afterwards walked among us, giving all a special darshan.

On Christmas morning, at five o'clock, the Western devotees were allowed to lead Nagar Sankirtan and we joined the procession around the ashram, singing carols and holding lighted candles. Afterwards Sai Baba stood on the balcony of His quarters to bless everyone. Later, at darshan, Sai Baba's students entertained us with carols and other Western songs, together with seasonal plays. Their excellent performances were enhanced by colourful costumes and seasonal humour. Then, in the early evening, a play by the children of devotees was performed in front of Swami, to rapturous applause. The day ended with Sai Baba giving a discourse, referring often to Jesus Christ and the meaning of Christmas. Here are three short extracts which convey only a small, but important, part of His Christmas message:

> Christmas is celebrated in innumerable places all over the world. Nowhere in the world is it done in the way it is celebrated here at Prasanthi Nilayam. People elsewhere may attend some church service and revel in drinking and dining parties but here people from many countries in the world, speaking many languages, following different faiths and cultures, assemble together unitedly, start the day with God's name and glory regardless of their differences, join in spending the day in carrying the message of Universal love. This is unity in diversity and true advaita (non-duality) in action.

> Christ taught people to love all beings and serve all with compassion. It is only by practising these ideals that one can truly celebrate His birthday. The Divinity within should be reflected in every action. The seat of Truth is in your heart. Worship means loving others with your full heart. You must live in love and lead a life of selfless service based on love. This is the only right way of celebrating the birth of Christ.

> The grace of God cannot be won through the gymnastics of reason, the contortions of yoga or denials of asceticism. Love alone can win it, love that needs no requital, love that knows no bargaining, love that is paid gladly as tribute to all living, love that is unwavering.

Joan and I, together with a few friends, were so overwhelmed by the whole Christmas experience at Prasanthi Nilayam that we felt we would like to celebrate our traditional English festivities in a similar way.

For Christmas 1993, we were fortunate enough to hire a boys' school over the holiday period which was, indeed, a most wonderful and memorable occasion. However, catering had not been provided and we sadly concluded that the school was not the most suitable venue for a future event. Despite having plenty of volunteers, the kitchen duties took up so much time that those involved were unable to fully participate in the activities.

The following Christmas, we were again unable to find accommodation with catering included. Instead, we decided to look for a venue available for a weekend during the summer holidays. We found the perfect location at a school near Newbury, which had formerly been a convent. We followed the daily ashram procedure of processional singing (the cloisters were ideal for this), and early morning and early evening devotional singing. The remainder of the day centred around meditation, lectures and spiritual workshops; we ended the evening with our own entertainment.

The first weekend proved so popular and successful that we visited the school again to inspect extra accommodation, looking to increase the numbers next time. Joan, Tom Dobson (a Committee member) and I, met the caretaker of the school and he showed us around. The additional accommodation proved suitable and enabled us to increase the capacity by a further 100 to a total of 300 for the next event.

As we were having a cup of tea with the caretaker at the end of the meeting, he suddenly looked up and said, '*Is that man who organises your event coming this year?*' We were somewhat taken aback and asked him if he meant the one in an orange robe whose photographs were in the main buildings that we used. He said, '*Yes*' and when we told him Sai Baba spent all His time in India the caretaker looked rather mystified. He then said, '*And the other man?*' We said, 'What other man?' and he described an old Indian man dressed in white, with a walking stick and what looked like a bobble hat (without the pom-pom) on his head. We all knew he meant Shirdi Sai Baba who was also an Avatar and had lived in the late nineteenth century.

Sri Sathya Sai Baba who, until now, I have called Sai Baba, had announced early in His life that He was one of a triple incarnation of Avatars, the first being Shirdi Sai Baba, then Himself and finally He would reincarnate as Prema Sai Baba. Incredibly, I just happened to have a photograph of Shirdi Sai Baba in my wallet, having been given it only the week before.

I showed it to the caretaker and he said, *'Yes that's him, such a lovely man.'* He continued, *'I was there by the theatre when this car drew up and your man* (Sathya Sai Baba) *got out of the car and walked up the steps to the entrance and was greeted by this old man* (Shirdi Sai Baba) *and they both went into the theatre together.'* We had to tell him that the old man, Shirdi Sai Baba, had died one hundred years ago. The caretaker was extremely puzzled and insisted that he had seen them both!

When we returned home Joan and I felt concerned about the caretaker, so I phoned to see if he was alright. I tried to reassure him, but although he sounded alright he obviously didn't understand. He had spoken to his wife after our visit and she remembered him telling her about it at the time. He repeated the story to me again.

This was wonderful news, as it demonstrated Sathya Sai Baba's omnipresence and that He was happy with the arrangements and activities for the weekend. It is well-known that He has simultaneously appeared in different parts of the world, in people's homes and at events. Nevertheless, we felt privileged to have been part of this special occurrence.

Life became even busier with our involvement in the UK Sai Organisation and by now, 1993, we were taking our own groups to see Sai Baba.

We visited Puttaparthi at least once a year and had new experiences each time. For this year's pilgrimage, in October, we settled on a smaller number in the group of about twenty. This enabled us to get to know each other more quickly starting, as usual, with a meeting a few weeks before leaving England.

On this visit the group seemed completely united and we were rewarded with an interview. We sat on the veranda outside the main building where the interviews took place. The senior officials of the organisation and long-term devotees had the honour of being seated here, near to Sai Baba, just in case He needed to speak to them about any ongoing projects.

Swami completed darshan which He ended by talking to some of the people on the veranda. As He walked close to us He almost touched me and I was aware of the most wonderful fragrance exuding from Him. During the interview, He spoke to us at length, asking and answering spiritual questions.

On my previous visit I had mentally asked Him for more self-confidence. In reply to a question about self-realisation He said that the first step was self-confidence. He repeated it, looking straight at me with a knowing look, adding, *'self-confidence leads to self-sacrifice and self-sacrifice leads to self-realisation.'* Later, in meditation, I received further clarification as follows:

Self-confidence – confidence in the *real* self (higher self).
Self-sacrifice – sacrifice the *little* self (ego).
Self-realisation – realisation of the *real* self (higher self).

Someone asked, 'How can I create a fountain of love in the heart?' Sai Baba replied, *'It is not a physical heart but a spiritual heart and the fountain of love with all the colours are there for you to create with. Love is natural and flows out from your heart.'* He stressed that it was a natural thing and not what you have to seek, as love is always there and flowing. Then, He pointed to His chest and said, *'Not physical heart but spiritual heart where beautiful colours flow from all the time, all the time.'*

Asked about meditation, Sai Baba explained:

> First is concentration, then contemplation.
> Meditation is beyond the senses: it lifts you into another dimension.
> You are acutely aware, but it is as if you are not there, like a dream.

He then spoke of the mind, saying how alive it is and that you cannot control it; but if you put it to work – at this point He put His finger on His top lip and said, *'This is where the mind can work.'* He breathed in with the right nostril saying, *'So'* (I AM) and out through the left nostril saying, *'Hum'* (THAT). *'You put the mind to work and think of God, "So Hum, So Hum, So Hum" and practice, practice, practice.'*

On another visit in October 1994 we did not have an interview but, nevertheless, it was still an important time for we all learned much and still had the wonderful experience of darshan. I particularly remember the eventful, to say the least, return journey to Bangalore.

There were sixteen of us in four taxis and everything was going well until we were stopped from going through one village because it was election time and the local Congress candidate had been kidnapped! We had to turn around and take a longer route, but at the next village a rock suddenly appeared in front of us which had been dislodged by the vehicle in front. Our driver could not avoid it; it ruined the engine and sump, leaving oil flowing all over the road.

Now, only three taxis, one of them being a converted van, to convey sixteen passengers. Later in the journey the van suffered the loss of its rear window. This meant that the passengers in front were impeded further by having the rear window on their laps and the ones at the back had to hold onto the luggage to stop it falling out. If that was not enough the last taxi developed a puncture and, yes, the spare tyre was flat. The driver disappeared with the spare wheel and was not seen again for a couple of hours when, fortunately, a replacement taxi arrived.

Somehow, we managed to arrive in Bangalore for a meal before making our way to the airport. To finish the day, our taxi ran out of fuel and the taxi following us bumped it from behind for some distance before finding a petrol station to fill up.

What a journey! We were all tested for patience and other virtues but the only thing for it was to laugh, and we did non-stop, when we were finally on our way again. We arrived at the airport in time to catch our flight home. Later we realised that Sai Baba had been playing one of His games with us, known as leelas.

Life is a game, play it.
Life is a challenge, meet it.
Life is a dream, realise it.
Life is a sacrifice, offer it.
Life is love, enjoy it.
(Sai Baba)

During our early pilgrimages, devotees sat on the sand floor in the darshan area of the ashram. A few years later the floor was concreted, but it was still open to the elements until the mid-1990s.

Just before the roof was built we were again at Puttaparthi. On one occasion we went for darshan while it was raining; Sai Baba, as usual, walked around wearing His orange robe. However, as He approached, it suddenly struck me that the gown was completely dry!

Surprisingly, we were called for an interview, although we had heard it said that Swami didn't give interviews when it was raining. In addition to our group there were a few other people present in the interview room, all soaked to the skin. One small Indian lady was sitting at the front and Sai Baba materialised a large, gold necklace for her, saying that it had belonged to Lakshmi (a Hindu goddess of wealth, fortune and prosperity: both material and spiritual).

We were all astounded at the size of the necklace, which must have been over two inches wide. Swami attempted to place it around her neck, but she was very embarrassed by her wet state. He took a large envelope from among the letters He had collected earlier, placed the necklace inside, and then handed it to her.

Astonishingly, even the hem of His gown, which had been dragged in the rain outside, had remained completely dry. This was extraordinary when compared with our dripping wet clothes.

The following memorable experience occurred during our visit to Sai Baba in 1995, but before relating it I must include a little background information. In the early 1960s, long before central heating became commonplace, Joan and I were living in our first house. During the winter most people had a coal fire in the living room, around which they would huddle to keep warm, and it was important that the door was kept closed to keep draughts out.

At this time a song called, 'Open the Door, Richard' was very popular. I was in the habit of leaving the door open at times, to the natural annoyance of Joan. When this happened, she would often sing the beginning of the song, changing the words to, 'close the door, Richard.' At Prasanthi Nilayam, when Sai Baba called people for interview, it was customary for Him to open the door, invite everyone in, close the door Himself and then put on the fan before sitting down on the only chair in the room.

On this occasion, we had been called for a group interview. Swami entered the room first, followed by Joan as she happened to be immediately behind him. He sat down and invited Joan to sit next to Him on a small stool, which we had never seen in the room before. The remainder of the group came in and sat on the floor as usual; I was last through the door. At that very moment Sai Baba looked at Joan, smiled with a knowing look on His face and started to sing, 'close the door, Richard.'

What an unbelievable thing to happen. It was over thirty years since we had lived in our first house and how He arranged for Joan to enter the interview room first and me last, I shall never know. Swami used to say He knew everything about our current lives and previous ones. He certainly proved the former to us on more than one occasion.

> I know everything that has happened to everybody in the past, everything that is happening now, and everything that will happen.
>
> *(Sai Baba)*

In April 1996, Joan and I travelled alone to see Sai Baba. We wanted to visit Kodaikanal, high up in the hills, where it was cooler at this time of year and where Sai Baba usually spent a few weeks due to the extreme heat on the lower ground.

When we arrived in India, Swami was at Whitefield, Bangalore, and it was already really hot. Rumours abounded that He would shortly leave for Kodaikanal, which was also a popular holiday resort with a large lake. Sure enough, He left a few days later and we followed, flying south to Madurai. From there we travelled by taxi up the steep hill, negotiating numerous hairpin bends.

It was a nerve-racking trip, but we arrived safely and found a small hotel where we were fortunate to obtain accommodation without having booked in advance. When we had occasion to complain about the damp bedsheets we were told this was normal, due to the cool, wet, climate in this area!

The view overlooking the lake, near Sai Baba's residence, was enchanting at dawn, with the mist rising and the sun coming through. After our first darshan we met some Russian friends, among them Galea, a lady who had lived in England for many years and her twin sister, Sofia, from St. Petersburg. They had brought a group from Russia which included some devotees we had met on previous visits to Prasanthi Nilayam.

That evening, Galea and Sofia extended an invitation to us to join their group. Joan and I were a little hesitant as we had previously found that, when additional people joined with one of our groups, the energy was not the same as the unity was missing. We explained that we did not wish to disrupt the energy and unity of their group. However, they were insistent so we said we would pray that evening and see what happened.

The next morning I was in the second row of the darshan line on the men's side, wearing the usual white trousers and tunic, but without any scarf denoting I was a member of a particular group. It was protocol for all group members to wear the same colour scarf to identify themselves and to help the service volunteers.

There I was, sitting away from the Russian group, next to people I did not know, when Sai Baba appeared in front of me and said, 'Russian group – go.'

I could hardly believe it. However, I stood up and waved to Joan and the others who walked over to the interview area. Swami spoke individually to the entire group and, when it was my turn, He jokingly said, 'You, half-Russian.' We felt honoured to be part of the group and it turned out to be entirely harmonious. We learned quite a lot about each other and our different ways of life with the group leaders acting as interpreters.

Once again, another example of Sai Baba knowing everything we had done and talked about.

> I know all that happens to all because I am in everyone. This current is in every bulb. I illumine every consciousness. I am the inner motivator in each one of you.
>
> *(Sai Baba)*

Sai Baba placed great stress on the importance of service. All Sai groups and centres throughout the world were encouraged to carry out group and individual service.

In the UK, each centre had a service coordinator to investigate, suggest and promote service projects. This generally worked well, both regionally and nationally. Over the years our own centre was involved in many activities.

Locally, we assisted disabled children to go horse riding. It was necessary for each child to be accompanied by one adult for the length of the riding lesson and, usually, there was a shortage of people to do this. We also helped in providing food for the homeless in Bristol, either by assisting in the soup kitchen or driving to certain locations to deliver sandwiches, soup and cakes made by our volunteers.

We undertook some indoor painting, street rubbish clearance and, occasionally, we did gardening for householders who were unable to do it themselves, due to age or ill health. One day, upon returning to our cars, we all experienced the beautiful aroma of vibhuti surrounding us in the open air. We agreed it was a sign of Sai Baba's omnipresence and, surely, a blessing on our service.

One of our longest-running projects was the formation of a junior Gateway Club at Portishead, for children with special needs. This was in the early 1990s and in collaboration with the community nurse for the area. With money from the charity Children in Need we arranged a weekend at a nearby holiday park, which was a great success. We have since wondered who received the most benefit from the club, the children or us, for it was a joy and privilege to spend an hour or so each week entertaining them.

Portishead was also the venue for an annual Sai Baba open day which was very popular, with approximately two hundred people attending. Food and drinks were served and many willing hands brought and prepared the refreshments. There were speakers, singers, musicians, devotional singing and other activities: everyone joined in.

Invariably, on these special occasions, those with the gift of clairvoyance told us they had seen Sai Baba during the day. It was again taken as a sign of His omnipresence and that He approved of the proceedings. This was later confirmed to us during an interview in India.

Whilst Joan and I did not 'see' Him in this way, there was always an overwhelming sense of love and togetherness felt by those attending. It was a similar feeling to that experienced in His presence at the ashram.

Nationally, apart from the Newbury weekends already mentioned, a new Sai choir was formed. We had great fun at rehearsals and were asked to sing at various functions in different parts of the country.

Once a month we visited an open prison to sing devotional songs with several of the Asian detainees, some of whom had heard of Sai Baba. Unfortunately, we caused great consternation one day when performing the Hindu ritual of aarti, using camphor (a by-product of the bark and wood of the kapur tree which burns with a bright flame). Used in India, the camphor is lit in a lamp at the end of worship and waved towards the deity; in our case this was a full-length picture of Swami. The ceremony is completed by turning and waving the flame in the direction of those present. Suddenly, we were startled by the fire alarm triggered by the smoke from the camphor. As you can appreciate, it quickly became very hectic in the room and surrounding area.

Surprisingly, we were still allowed to visit the prison – but only if we left the camphor at home!

Looking back over the years I wonder how Joan and I managed to fit everything in, but in serving others self is forgotten and the grace of God takes over, giving joy in all that is undertaken.

Sai Baba made many references to service in His discourses and I have chosen a few of His most memorable ones:

> Hands that serve are holier than lips that pray.
> Love all, serve all; help ever, hurt never.
> Service is worship. Each act of service is a flower placed at the feet of God.
> Service is the first step along the spiritual path.
> Small minds select narrow roads; expand your mental vision and take to the broad road of helpfulness, compassion and service.
> Love lives by giving and forgiving; self lives by getting and forgetting.

After my retirement from work at the end of 1996, we planned to take a group to see Sai Baba the following January. Joan and I intended to follow this with some sightseeing in Bangalore and then a visit to Malaysia to see friends in Penang. Our friends had previously spent a few years in Bristol, one of them attending university, and throughout their stay were members of our local Sai centre.

Our visit to Prasanthi Nilayam turned out to be rather challenging as several of the group became ill, mainly with tummy trouble and chest infections. Unfortunately, one lady suffered a different but very serious problem and needed to go into hospital in Bangalore. Fortuitously, we happened to have a medical doctor in our group who accompanied us in the taxi.

The doctor and I stayed for a few days in Bangalore, while Joan remained in the ashram to look after our group. In Indian hospitals it was normal to provide one's own helpers, usually family members, to generally look after the patient and do some of the work that, in England, nurses would do. Two of our younger lady members accompanied us to provide this help, and a rota was set up for the other ladies in the group who volunteered their services. This continued for about ten days until I was able to arrange an escorted flight home for the patient, through the insurance company.

Joan and I were very grateful to those in the group who had given up valuable time away from their pilgrimage to give service at the hospital, but we knew they were only too pleased to volunteer. The remainder of the group were fit and well when the time came for their departure. Although we all experienced difficulties it was agreed that much had been learned from the visit.

After seeing the group aboard the plane Joan, and I relaxed at our hotel but, unfortunately, although I had been lucky to always avoid illness on these trips, I succumbed to the dreaded Delhi belly for a couple of days and couldn't make the planned visits to the sights of Bangalore. However, I recovered in time to catch the plane to Penang, arriving at the holiday resort to a wonderful greeting from our friends who quickly took us to their apartment. We spent a few days sightseeing with them but found the temperature so hot that we moved on to the Cameron Highlands, knowing that our friends would join us later. The weather here was more like British weather, including the rain which accompanied the lower temperature.

The driver who took us to our apartment was, by chance, a Sai Baba devotee and, later, he introduced us to a newly-formed Sai group in the Highlands. We subsequently visited the group, sharing some of our experiences, and they were so pleased to show us the vibhuti that had appeared overnight on one of their pictures of Sai Baba.

We shared a few days with our friends in the Cameron Highlands before catching a bus to Kuala Lumpur, again staying with Sai devotees. This introduction had been made and organised by a Sai colleague from London. We were thankful for their generous hospitality, which we were able to return a year later when they visited relatives in England and stayed with us to attend one of the Sai open days in Portishead.

Unluckily, while in the Highlands I developed a severe pain in my shoulder. A chiropractor, another Sai devotee, gave me treatment saying I had a trapped nerve and it would take a long time to heal. Unfortunately, I was unable to attend all the meetings in Kuala Lumpur but I did visit one lady's house whose shrine was, literally, covered in vibhuti, as were two or three photos of Swami. Sai Baba confirmed to some of His devotees that He was responsible for the manifestation of vibhuti on His photos. At the end of our holiday we stopped in Bangalore to have one last darshan before returning home.

The trapped nerve in my shoulder did, indeed, take several months to heal and I was reminded of it in 2015 when I again suffered from the same problem. This time I had three treatments from my osteopath without any significant progress and I feared several months on the sideline once more.

Shortly afterwards, I received a message from Joan, through a clairvoyant, giving the name of our former General Practitioner who was now pursuing a career in sports medicine. The clairvoyant also said that I should have acupuncture from him. In fact, five years previously he had given me a short session of this therapy for a lower back problem.

Eventually, I managed to contact him and subsequently received two half-hour sessions; my trapped nerve was cured almost immediately.

It is unusual for clairvoyants to give surnames, but in this case the doctor's full name was given. This to me was another altogether remarkable incident which proved that our loved ones in spirit do everything they can, when appropriate, to provide help and guidance for us.

We spent a second Christmas at Prasanthi Nilayam in 1997. Our party arrived early in December as the ashram always became very busy in the lead-up to Christmas.

It was compulsory for all groups to attend an orientation meeting the morning following arrival. On this occasion the lecturer stressed that if we wanted an interview the leaders should draw attention to themselves by, for instance, jumping up and down and calling out for an interview which, incidentally, was contrary to the rules of the ashram.

Attention-seeking was not my style, so I decided to write a letter to Swami. I explained I was not an extrovert and that my way was the quiet way, through love and peace. I wrote about several things, including an interview for the group, adding that I was requesting the interview because we were of one mind and proud to bear the name of the United Kingdom. Sai Baba took my letter the next day and I hoped this was significant, for one could never guarantee an interview; there were always so many people wanting the same thing.

About a week later at darshan we were again fortunate to be near the front, all in a row, and Swami walked straight past, seeming to ignore me, and moved further along the line. He suddenly stopped and asked our last man in the row, 'How many?' and then said, 'go.'

The atmosphere in the interview room was electric. Baba was talking to us and we, in turn, asked questions. He said that we were living in a dream world, but when in the interview room with Him that was Reality.

Swami always emphasised the importance of the five main human values of love, truth, peace, right action and non-violence, the tenet of His teachings. In answer to a question on His Education in Human Values programme (EHV), taught in all His schools and in many others around the world, He replied: '3*HV: Heart, Head, Hands.*' '*Practice what you preach, what your heart feels, what your head understands and then you work with your hands.*' He continued, '*The spirit of love is spirituality, the split of love is science.*' '*Love is life source, not life force.*'

I asked a question about the relationship between karma (law of cause and effect) and one's intended life plan. He replied simply, *'Love'*, then explained that love as attachment is not pure love as it is attachment to the body. He added:

> Truth is the embodiment of love.
> Peace is the embodiment of love.
> Truth is a value, but what is truth without words?
> Peace is a value, but where is peace without action and love?
> So, 3HVs: Heart, Head, Hands, and the end of education is Character.

Someone asked why we became tired very quickly compared to Him. With His customary play on words, He replied, *'Interest: if you have interest you are not tired, but if you do not then you are "into rest", not interest.'*

He continued, *'You are three people*:

> Mind – the one people think you are.
> Body – the one you think you are.
> Atma (God) – the one you really are.'

I asked how we could help with His mission and He said, *'Not my mission, our mission.'*

The words *'our mission'* became even more relevant for me last year when I again attended the Omega Circle. Sai Baba spoke to me through the medium and told me that the knowledge He possessed, and of which I was now aware, was important for humanity. He went on, *'I know you looked up to me but I was your brother; it is important that you realise that within you is what I have, because I have given it to you.'* He finished by saying that all His tricks and garlands were to show His followers that He was Divine and that God incarnate was within everyone.

Sai Baba explained His mission in 1968, in His birthday discourse, and it included:

> To establish righteousness.
> To re-establish you in the ways of peace, truth and love.
> To instruct all in the essence of the Vedas (ancient Indian scriptures); to shower on all this precious gift, to protect the ancient wisdom and preserve it.
> To spread happiness.
> To realise that the Lord is within you.

He continued the interview with, '*See good, think good, be good; hear good, speak good, do good.*' He repeated '*think good*' pointing to His heart and then said, '*G-O-O-D – take out the zero and you have God.*' Lastly, He said, '*Love is everything; start the day with love, fill the day with love, end the day with love.*'

We were not given vibhuti packets at the end of the interview, as normally happens, but He said that He would see us again. We did not take this too literally, although we hoped for another interview, as we knew that saying this could mean He would see us in darshan or on our next visit.

The next day devotees from Leicester were attending their first group darshan and were sitting close to us. Swami passed by, not speaking to me, but appeared to be standing between the two groups as the Leicester party stood up to go for an interview. They had reached the veranda before Swami sent them back saying it was the wrong group. Before we realised it, He had sent His attendant to us and so, incredibly, we were called for another interview.

As we entered the interview room He playfully pretended to smack Maurice, a group member, and I because we hadn't stood up for the interview as the Leicester group had. He began by saying that He was very, very, happy. We were again able to ask questions and someone said, 'Is free will an illusion?' The response was, '*Yes, in essence there is only one free will and that is the Divine free will. Free will only in God, not in person* (body), *but choice is everywhere.*'

Speaking of Jesus Swami said:

First – Jesus was a messenger of God.
Second – He felt he was Son of God.
Third – He realised I and my Father are One.

In Sanskrit he further explained:

Dvaita (duality) – I am in the light.
Vishista Advaita (qualified Oneness) – The light is in me.
Advaita (Oneness) – I am the light.

He was asked if Jesus atoned for the sins of the whole world on the cross and He answered, *'No; priests and politicians made that up.' 'Jesus heard on the cross, "All are One, my dear Son; be alike to everyone."'*
'All faiths have same principles; jewels are many, but gold is one.' 'God is One; goal is one.'

He then held up a handkerchief, saying, *'Cloth? No, this is bundle of thread.'*

First – Cotton.
Second – Thread.
Third – Cloth.
Three are One.

Suddenly, Sai Baba looked directly at Joan and said, *'Swami only gives; not a beggar. I want only love, love, love.'*

This statement was so meaningful to us because we were aware that Swami didn't wish His devotees to promote Him in any way or ask for money. At this time He had started the Water Project, bringing clean water to thousands of people in Andhra Pradesh and we had encountered someone promoting a scheme, using Swami's name, to collect money for it.

Baba had categorically said that no charge should ever be made for meetings or projects bearing His name. This had always been our experience and practice when attending meetings, or arranging them for the Sai Organisation. Money for projects had always been freely given, without any appeal or request.

Swami also confirmed in the interview that He had been present at the Newbury meeting with the caretaker, mentioned earlier in the book. He explained that He was always at this type of meeting because they were concentrated groups adding, with a smile, the acronym, '*CIA Constant Integrated Awareness.*'

Later, He was asked about body, mind and spirit and said that there was a distinction. '*Body is materialisation; mind is vibration; spirit is radiation.*' He continued by describing three types of teachers: those who complain, those who explain and those who inspire. '*First be, then tell and do.*'

Following the question, 'How can I improve my spiritual life?' Swami replied, '*Only through love: whatever you do, do with love. That is spirituality!*'

Finally, as He sang '*Love is my form*' to us all, Joan said His eyes seemed to come right into her body. Unbelievably His face became a multitude of lights and across His forehead was a rainbow. She said that it was beyond belief and almost too powerful to keep looking. What an experience!

Afterwards we realised that we had been in the interview room for over forty-five minutes, when most interviews were usually half that time. We felt very blessed to have been granted two interviews at this special time of year, not just because of the length of time we had been given but because of the intensity of Swami's care, humour, teachings and love, together with His demonstration of omnipresence.

We were still heavily involved with the Sai Organisation, locally and nationally, when, in November 1998, we made our last visit to Prasanthi Nilayam, for Swami's birthday and the World Conference for Centre Presidents. Whilst the birthday celebrations took place in the Hillview Stadium, with hundreds of thousands of people attending, Joan and I were fortunate to be in the ashram for the conference. Altogether, one hundred and thirty-nine countries were represented at both events.

The World Conference was a memorable experience, affording everyone the opportunity to mix, discuss and enjoy the company of devotees from all over the world. There were workshops and lectures, but the highlight of the event was the inspirational valedictory discourse given by Sai Baba. He spoke for over an hour and covered many topics including man's ego, truth, speaking from the heart, happiness and sorrow, transformation, unity in diversity, cleansing and purity, dreams, work; considering all forms as divinity and love.

The following extracts from His discourse illustrate these points:

> Man will enjoy bliss only when he gets rid of ego and attachment.
>
> Mind is the source of happiness and sorrow. So, conquer the mind. Conquering the mind will lead you to the state of equanimity, wherein you treat the dualities alike.
>
> Welcome sorrow, just as you welcome happiness. In fact, the happiness that you derive out of pleasure is negligible compared to the happiness that results from difficulties.
>
> What is required today is transformation, which can be effected by questioning oneself, 'Who am I?' Once you know the answer to this and reach the state of transformation, you need no further spiritual practices.

God is in everyone. We should visualise this unity in diversity and try to experience it. Consider this as your chief goal.

Those who speak from the heart speak the truth; others, whose speech does not come from the heart, speak untruth to suit the occasion. Your words should emanate from the heart.

Man has to be cleansed by the process of refinement to get rid of all the bad qualities and regain his resplendent pristine purity.

Dreams are reflections of the subconscious mind. Dreams are the reflection, reaction and resound of that which is within you. The same does not apply to the dreams in which Swami appears. Swami appears in dreams only when He wills it and not when you want.

Do not make any distinction between God and yourself, His work and your work. Work with the conviction that you and God are one.

You may undertake any type of spiritual pursuit, but love wholeheartedly. Love can eradicate any type of disease and act as a panacea for all afflictions. You must, in the first instance, develop love. This can be possible if you believe that God is the embodiment of Love. How can you develop love when you do not believe that God is the embodiment of Love?

If one cultivates love, one need not undertake any other spiritual pursuits.

Consider all people to be the forms of divinity. Have faith that God is in all. That pleases me the most. Refrain from doing that which causes grief to others even if it were to give you happiness. Do unto others as you would like to be done by. Help ever; Hurt never. Help everybody. Do not harm or hurt anyone. Do not develop ill feelings toward anybody. Even if people were to hurt you or curse you, do not refrain from loving them. This is the main point of Swami's teachings. That is what Swami expects of you.

I am pleased with whatever you undertake with purity of heart; I desire only the purity of your heart. With pure love in your heart, you may undertake any type of service. Have total faith in Swami's words, implicitly obey His commands.

We were in awe after hearing these words, having felt Swami's Divine love within us as His aura reached everyone present. We left Prasanthi Nilayam in a state of bliss, with love in our hearts and with a will to work even harder in the days ahead.

In June 1999, we had planned to visit David and Ann Jevons who had moved to Canada, having sold the main Ramala house in Glastonbury, leaving a friend to live-in and manage the smaller building. (I mentioned David and Ann earlier).

A few days before we were due to leave I became extremely unwell with a mystery illness and was eventually rushed to hospital for an exploratory operation. It transpired that I had peritonitis due to a burst appendix and the operation that day came just in time. Apparently, my appendix had not been in the normal position and that is why the doctors couldn't at first diagnose the problem.

Upon hearing of this, our dear friends, Arthur and Poppy Hillcoat from Australia, invited Joan and I for a visit to help my recuperation. We had a wonderful time with them and meeting some of their friends. One evening we were honoured to meet Howard Murphet who was staying nearby. Howard was very well-known to Sai friends as he was one of the first foreign devotees to visit Prasanthi Nilayam in 1966, at a time when it was extremely difficult to travel there.

In his younger days, Howard served in the British Eighth Army during the Second World War and later was in charge of the British Press Section at the Nuremberg War Trials. He first heard about Sai Baba when attending a Theosophical Society meeting near Madras and, subsequently, had many amazing experiences in Swami's presence. Howard related these in his books, *Sai Baba Man of Miracles* and *Sai Baba Avatar*. Having read them we were keen to be introduced to Howard, who was now in his mid-nineties.

The meeting, in Queensland, had been arranged as a birthday celebration for Howard and for those with birthdays around that time. As it was my birthday on the day of the meeting I felt very happy to be given this special treat. In a tribute, Howard was described as one of those few people who really stood out in life. He made such an impression on hearts and souls and people had been so moved by him, by his example, by his stories, by his sweetness, by his love of animals, and by his infinite view of spirituality.

I recorded his talk and feel it is worth including in full to show his humility and humour, and because he has put something extra into the meaning of why God created man:

> I want to thank you for what you said; it was a good piece. I wish I was worthy of it but I'm not. Nevertheless, it was lovely to hear and there's no doubt about it I feel tonight that we in this room are all one. Would to God we could feel that with everyone in the world, then Swami's task would be over and he could go back to where he belongs but he's got a long, long job ahead because of us difficult children. But these sort of gatherings bring us together, give us memories of love of everybody around when we really felt as one, and as One with Swami himself, God Himself.
>
> I don't think I want to say any more unless there's something else you want me to talk about. I will say this, however; that last year in particular I felt there was great unity but, beware, for where you feel great unity some ego will pop up and spoil the harmony. But let that not worry us, we must always rise above that and set an example to everybody else. We must do it; can't expect anybody else to set the example of love and Oneness because only in that way can we learn the lesson we are here for. Until we learn it we'll go on with the joys and pains.
>
> So, even that is something we must do. We must gain always a deeper understanding of God and of ourselves because we are all forms through which God is expressing Himself and gaining experience. That's why we're here; God wanted to experience through all of us individually, unique experiences of each one. So, we do have a purpose on earth, not only for us to gain our highest spiritual wisdom, happiness and continual bliss throughout eternity ourselves, but to give God the chance of experiencing lives through each of us. That's the other side of it.
>
> So, thank you all and particularly the Queensland people and this group. I've always loved coming up here.

I am mindful of Baba's well-known sayings, so in accord with Howard's talk:

> I have separated Myself from Myself, so that I may love Myself.
> See in Me yourself, for I see Myself in you all.
> You are My life, My breath, My soul.
> When I love you I love Myself.
> When you love yourselves you love Me.
> My beloved ones, you are My own self.

After returning from Australia, Joan and I felt that Sai Baba was encouraging us to widen our spiritual horizons. We had already started reading the book *A Course in Miracles* (ACIM), received as a channelling by Helen Schucman, assisted by William Thetford, which describes the impermanence of human life and expounds that everything in life is not what it appears to be.

The following year, 2000, we were inspired to visit America to study a course built around the book. This was to be a unique experience for us and we were expecting to stay for three months.

A typical day started with readings from ACIM and this was followed by the assembled company awaiting the arrival of the facilitator. Many people lived locally and took part in the daily meetings when he usually gave a talk taken from the workshop section of the Course. After this, a different genre of music was played each day, followed by most people taking to the floor. Dancing ensued with hands held high above the head, the participants apparently feeling a connection between their inner self and all life; the aim appeared to be self-realisation.

A variety of recreational activities were available. To keep costs down, the residents were expected to carry out general housekeeping duties together with a spell in the kitchen, when appropriate. We soon became accustomed to the routine; Joan particularly enjoyed the art classes and singing and became a member of the choir. It sounded idyllic, and in many ways it was. However, there were one or two niggling situations but these were set aside when the facilitator gave his illuminating talks.

In the evenings we had the opportunity to visit another location, a few miles away, where hymns and beautiful music were played. Again, people went onto the dance floor to experience their connection within and it seemed several were, indeed, reaching a state of ecstasy. Whilst enjoying the music and togetherness we did not have the unusual or special feelings that others appeared to be having. In fact, on one occasion, it was suggested to us that we should fake it! That did not go down well with us and, following one or two other incidents, it made us wonder if this was the right place to be.

It did not take long for things to come to a head one morning when the facilitator announced that he had lost a court case, preventing him from publishing his material under the name of ACIM. He sounded as though he was in despair and asked for any suggestions. Well, being a rather reserved person I was surprised to have one of those moments when something within made me stand up (just as I did in the presence of Sai Baba). I proposed that he could write everything in his own name because the quality of his talks and teachings was excellent. To our utter astonishment he talked me down in a most unloving manner and seemed to be critical of both Joan and I.

After the meeting we wanted to leave immediately but, of course, we first had to rearrange our flight as we were only two months into our stay. I contacted the airline who made arrangements for us to fly home the following day. The return journey went so smoothly that it seemed to us that we had been playing our parts and followed the script.

Subsequently, we began studying with friends the works of Joel Goldsmith and the Eastern spiritual philosophy of advaita (nonduality) and we read together books by Nisargadatta Maharaj, Sri H.W.L. Poonja, Gangaji, Adyashanti and others. We met weekly, reading and discussing as we went, and often remarked that the teachings bore a striking resemblance to those of Sai Baba. We really enjoyed those times and some of the words like 'nobody's home' still make us laugh today. It certainly gave us an insight into understanding the meaning of the Oneness of all life.

The meetings continued throughout Joan's illness until it became impossible to carry on. Nevertheless, our friends and others made regular visits to Joan for as long as possible.

My book, *Light the Way*, explains how and when communication with Joan and those on the 'other side' began. Since then, my life has been unimaginably exciting and interesting. The channelling has increased, both in circle meetings and visits to friends in different parts of the country, when meditating at their request.

It culminated in August 2016, after I was invited to St. Petersburg by my Russian friends Galea, and Sofia who kindly provided accommodation. This enabled me to experience life closer to the Russian people than one would normally expect when on holiday. I found them very courteous, friendly and helpful.

My host, Sofia, and those I met at prearranged meetings, couldn't do enough for me and helped make my visit both memorable and fruitful. The love extended was palpable and shown in many ways, such as the refreshments which were always brought to the meetings by guests and included, on one occasion, a delicious mushroom pie made from wild mushrooms collected from the forest.

I was able to record most of the channelling that took place during my time in Russia and, on one occasion, I was humbled and privileged to have received inspired words from Sai Baba. (See Chapter 7, page 208).

Following my return from Russia I continued to expand the channelling to friends, groups and the three circles I am now involved with. Some of my channelling has been included in the later chapters of the book. On one occasion, when illness prevented a circle meeting taking place, it was decided that two of us participate by using the telephone, set to loudspeaker mode thus enabling events to be recorded as usual. Our spirit friends still gave messages through us and channelling took place. Remarkably, they also caused uncontrollable laughter from us for a few minutes during the meeting.

Now, to the present, and with the future unwritten... At this stage in my journey I claim no specific spiritual heritage, but I feel I am now being used in a more general way to pass on important teachings from the next dimension, including channellings from my collective guide, Joyful One, and, occasionally, from a source in the higher realms. As I have previously explained, I have no idea beforehand who is going to speak through me, nor what is to be said. I am only aware of the immediate words given, not the whole talk, and I am always eager to hear the recordings. I have no expectations but I surrender myself with the utmost trust to these loving friends.

My spiritual adventures will continue, so the time has come to call a halt in order that this book may be completed. I have enjoyed immensely reliving my experiences and I hope this selection will strike a chord within and resonate with you.

Chapter Two

Two-Way Communication

I have included in this Chapter a further exchange of letters with Joan, choosing those which I feel best reflect my spiritual progress and something of everyday living since writing *Light the Way*. Again, as the letters were coming through I was not completely conscious of what was being said. I can best describe our communication as channelling on a soul level.

Then follow extracts from my channelled talks at circle meetings:

Firstly, Joan speaks of some earthly memories, her work now, and comments on Oneness.

Secondly, there are questions from circle members, together with the answers given by spirit.

To conclude, sitters in circle were one day asked by spirit to comment on the I AM and I give their inspired answers.

14 August 2014

My darling Rich

I love you my precious. You have had some moments in the last few days when you have been a little emotional. I was with you then, as I am with you always when you need me. It has been a little while since I last spoke to you like this, but that does not mean I haven't wanted to. You were going through a certain stage that required you to appear to be on your own, but that is now over and I am here with you encouraging you to write.

You were, and we, too, were in great form on Tuesday and you found the words flowing easily. You handled it all very well and were the perfect channel.

You know I want to tell you all about the future but I have my hands tied, so to speak. Rest assured things will all fall into place before long and you will appear to be carried along without any effort. Your imagination is not too off the mark; you will be involved with other people. You will be travelling and you will be speaking, channelling, as you go. More than that I cannot say at the moment, but I will be with you, by your side, encouraging you every step of the way.

You will also become busier on the healing front and you will see and hear things to assist you. So, relax and let us take you with us on the next step of your exciting life story. Feel me, and see me on your travels. I am by your side and, together, we will fulfil our planned time together on earth and between the two worlds.

My love for you is endless. God bless, my darling.

Joan

20 May 2015

My darling Joan

I love you so much. I have missed writing to you recently, but I still talk to you and think of you. This bug has been a bit restrictive for me; I'm not used to being under the weather like this but I am getting there with your help. It's been an interesting time but you have still come through to me. In circle, you give wonderful words; all of you, together. I have not been myself so I assume you have not given me other articles at different times. However, although it doesn't sound like it, I feel much better now and ready to resume my channelling, subject to you all wanting to continue.

I thank you for all you do in the background; you have helped me so much recently. I do love you and think of you, remembering our wonderful times together. I also think of the times in the early days when I could have been different, but I didn't have the advantage of experience in those days. I was so lucky to have met you when I did and you were my guide and support. We were truly a delightful pair together, each supporting the other. I treasure our moments together from those first early days to the latter days, when it was so difficult for you.

I love you and feel you here with me now, just as we were together so many times. The house should be empty without your physical presence, but it doesn't feel empty for I know you are here so often. I am very fortunate to have a wonderful partner, even now on the other side of the veil. I am lucky to have the knowledge and experience that you are with me, helping me in the difficult times as well as in the good times. I appreciate so much you coming through when I am with friends channelling.

It has been a while since I talked to you like this and I have missed it, for I appreciate our closeness at times like this. Thank you, my precious darling one. I love you.

Richard

24 May 2015

I missed you, darling Rich.

Hearing from you is always a treat, whether it be verbally or writing to me. I am with you whenever you need me. You have had a difficult time recently; however, you kept going as you always did. You have a strong will and strong constitution. You try to help whenever possible and you have offered yourself openly to do the Lord's work.

We have spent wonderful times together at the feet of the Lord. What a privilege for us. Now, your pathway is a little different, but you are aware of the Presence within. This Presence can go by any name. I know you are feeling the Presence now; it is filling your whole body, your whole being. Relax and open up to Him and to us.

Nothing, no experience, is wasted. You will be all the stronger now and we are surrounding you with love and strength as you prepare yourself for the work ahead. So, continue meeting your God, and all of us, at this early hour; it is so peaceful and communication is good at this time.

I love you, my darling. I, too, treasure my memories of us together and I still cuddle you, sit next to you and walk with you, especially when you are not sure what to do and when you are helping others. Keep in contact, my precious, by word or like this; just think of me and I am there. We had such a loving relationship and still do. God bless you, my ever-loving friend.

Joan

1 October 2015

Hello, my precious

Yes, I am with you. I am surrounding you, holding your hand like you used to hold mine, giving you healing like you used to give me; just giving you a top-up of love.

I'm so proud of what you are doing. You are following your inspirations and not ducking out of opportunities, which not long ago would have passed you by. You have more than come out of your shell, although that term is not fair on you. It just illustrates how far you have come, what you are capable of and what you will be doing.

We spent many birthdays together; yours and mine and the boys. I know how important birthdays are to you. (Channel's birthday today). You may have said that it is just like any other day but, within, there was something special and there still is for you.

I am so pleased to be sharing it with you my darling. I love you and always will. I want the best for you as always and I know that we are still together, hand in hand, going through your wonderful life which is expanding and in which you will be so fulfilled.

I will pop in again during the day and evening, for I am never far away from you. We are still like twin souls: 'your other half', as Sai Baba said. Have a wonderful day, darling. Think of me and we will spend some time together. I love you.

Joan

28 November 2015

Hello, my precious

I love you so very much. You mean the world to me, my darling, and I wonder how I have coped all this time without your physical presence. You've had a part in some interesting experiences for me recently, and I know you do so much for me from where you are. I am sure I will understand more in time, but I would like to see you like others do.

I am so fortunate to be given words to speak by you and your friends, and sometimes by you direct, but I don't 'see' yet, other than in a dream. What about the Sunday circle? It sounds as though it will be permanent, although obviously not so frequent as the Tuesday one. No doubt there is a unique purpose for it and I must say it was most enjoyable last week. I now seem to be more involved in healing and counselling over the telephone. Is this all part of the extra work I am and will be doing?

I close my eyes and feel you next to me, my darling; I see light and feel so close to you. We are only apart physically and when I let go and think of you, you are there. You said more people would be asking about spirit and the afterlife but I am always surprised by who raises the questions; two in the last week! I know you must be guiding and helping me to give the right words and ideas. Please continue to; it seems so natural at the time.

It's wonderful to be talking to you, as always, and takes me right back to when we first met. What fantastic memories. I shall go to sleep tonight thinking about them, and especially sensing you close.

Goodnight, my precious. I love you.

Rich

20 December 2015

Hello, my precious Rich

I wanted to say how much I love you on our special day. (Our wedding anniversary). I gave them all a message in circle today so I am now giving you yours, in the privacy of just you and me. I have been working with you recently so that I could come through both circles. You have come such a long way to have the confidence to keep going and give such full messages and teachings. I am very proud of you for the discipline you have shown to bring such clarity and fluency in your channelling.

We have worked hard with you each morning, and sometimes at night, to reach the current standard. Obviously, when I speak through you I cannot let any sign of emotion come through as you, too, need to be free of that. I know you cannot believe how well it flowed today, and no wonder. You and I were overcome with emotion hearing those beautiful, familiar songs tonight. They were tears of happiness, with a tinge of sadness that we were not physically together on this important day.

The world is your oyster, my darling. Let go and follow your heart and we will continue to work together, even if you think it is someone else with you giving the words. My world on earth was you, and from your thoughts you felt the same for me. It is wonderful being with you as you try to remember those fantastic experiences with Swami. It's great you have completed another experience and you will find they will flow again with our help.

We are still so in tune, you and I, as you picked up my signal to write to you when you were nearly asleep. Retire now then, my love, with my breath and kisses sending you to sleep. Goodnight, my precious partner and best friend. God bless you. I love you.

Joan

28 August 2016

Hello, my precious

I love you Rich, beyond description. I have been with you so closely for the last ten days or so. From the time you started your journey to Russia to your return home, I have hardly left your side. I know you felt me at times and I shared with you that euphoric feeling when you were working there. How did you like what we arranged for you and all your new and old friends? You responded so well, having been prepared for a long time now to become such a good channel. You will find we are ready to talk through you more and more.

I held you and slept with you in the flat, especially when you were on your own. You helped so many people, more than you can imagine, and you gave of yourself, your time and love, and it is no wonder that you felt that wondrous feeling within. As you said in an email, life will never be the same again for you. I have seen you so confident and assured which, together with your loving manner, has made you into a very desirable marriage partner for someone. I feel as though I am falling in love with you all over again, my darling, and if I was on the earth now I would be first in line.

I know you have been very busy, and will continue to be, but take time for you in-between the work. I am so proud of you and know you will complete your special pathway in this lifetime. Enjoy your day tomorrow; we will be there! Relax for your few days away; you will be ready to work when required. Looking ahead, you will soon be ready to work on the book again and you will be given all the help you need.

So, be at One in all you do; work, rest and play, and you will feel a continuous connection with All That Is. Thank you for making this time to listen and write.

I love you.

Joan

30 December 2016

My darling Rich

Oh, how I wished to put my arms around you today, watching that film which touched you so much.

I love you, precious, more each day. Didn't we have a marvellous anniversary? I thought you would like me coming through in both circles. You channelled very well considering the experience of holding a one-to-one circle with Pam over the telephone.

I just wanted to speak to you direct tonight as it was not possible at Christmas. You are picking up the right vibes for your talk in Cornwall. I will help you to prepare the rest: not much, as you will speak the words without reading them on the day and we will come through and talk via you in the meditation. It will all be fine and you will enjoy it.

How do you like my input for the new kitchen? I am sure you are not surprised that I helped you choose it. You will love the finished article.

Now, about the book: just relax and let it come through. You will know what to put into the book and how to arrange it. You have the title now; it will be great and you will enjoy putting it together. There is no rush; all will work out at the right time.

You are feeling more sensitive now, due to all the meditation and being open to the Great Spirit and all life. You will experience more than you can imagine in 2017 and I will be with you every step of the way. You are ready for the real channelling which you will be so pleased and honoured to be part of. Just let go and trust, which you do, and all will be perfect.

I am thrilled that you are picking up thoughts and guidance. Don't ever be afraid to say anything or do anything when prompted, which you are beginning to do more and more.

Don't worry about your age; you will be given all the strength you need. Just keep balancing your life with leisure, sport and rest, when appropriate.

Oh, it is wonderful to be talking to you now and being with you.

I like it that you keep putting a clean sheet on my bed. I am there beside you more than you think. I love you with all my heart and soul and will continue to be by your side.

You are feeling my love and my spirit next to you now. Rest in the love which is so pure and comes from the Father, Swami, Christ; all One! As you reach out to me I shower you with kisses and bliss.

All my love, forever.

Joan

22 January 2017

My dearest Joanie

 I love you more than I ever thought possible. Talk about absence making the heart grow fonder: absence of the body, but not of the spirit. I am so fortunate that you are close to me, especially when I need you, and you help me in so many ways.

 You've inspired me to make the right choices in the new kitchen and it looks perfect: much better than I would have imagined. It's been a strange time and a bit difficult not being able to settle during the day, but that's nearly done. I can then settle down and be in touch more than ever. I feel at a crossroads, although I have no reason to say that other than the disruption of the past few weeks.

 So, I am open to you and all life and will do what is in my heart. I know you are guiding me so I will keep on being in touch. I have been given so much in circle and at other times. Whatever happens, I love you my darling, more and more. I miss your physical presence and hope to be more at one with you.

 Thanks for all the help today. I look forward to seeing you in my dreams. I will love you forever. God bless you, my darling.

Rich

28 January 2017

Rich

    Yes, I do hear you: I hear you when you call me, for I love you. My love for you is complete; my love is unswerving, unconditional, and I would do anything to help but I must allow you to live your life with all its opportunities. With every experience you meet I hope you feel me close, for we are one *in the moment.*

    You have said you feel at a crossroads; I would rather say you have reached a stepping-stone. The interruption in your life with your new kitchen, our new kitchen, has been good, if not pleasant at times for you. You can now go forward in life with love.

    You will be helped in Cornwall. You have done the preparatory work and you will know how much to say, for you will be inspired. Just connect and you will feel love all around you.

    As your life moves up a notch you will know when to rest and when to be in contact with us and you will see life unfolding in a way not imagined by you. You don't need faith; you have the knowing that God is within you, that God is you and you are God. You will take that knowledge with you wherever you go and you will feel spirit about you, for you are such a willing warrior on the road of service to your fellow man.

    So, be happy; be confident we are with you. Take me with you as you journey today and I will enjoy the weekend with you.

    I love you darling, God bless you.

Joan

25 June 2017

Hello darling Rich

Yes, I am here at one with you again. No need for words, but I will say some to give you support and all my love. We were there for each other on earth; you listened to me so much when I wanted to talk, and I listened to you. You didn't appear to need as much help but everyone does need help on earth. It is natural, for the Great Spirit has given everybody the ability to converse with one another, to be aware of close one's needs.

So, I am aware that you are working hard at the moment, putting what you consider appropriate on the computer for possible use in the book. Read them all from a third-party point of view and then decide whether they should be included. I will be with you and help you to decide, also with one or two things which don't quite make sense to you. We will go over it again and your mind will have clarification.

Oh, my darling, I am holding you close, cuddling you as you used to cuddle me.

We keep giving you words about not worrying and, if you follow that advice, difficult though it is, you will find that there was no need to worry. You go forth with a happy attitude, helping people whenever you can and listening when it is needed. You go the extra mile and we do the same for you. Open up to me, to the Great Spirit, to all who can help when you are in need and, indeed, whenever you think as you do now of the Oneness between us all. I used to say there is only One, that the 'me', the little I, did not exist.

Take care, my love; you still have much to do. Not everything given to you in words has to be kept or transcribed but, you will know the ones to keep.

Last night you suddenly felt at one with me and I felt the same, my precious. Whilst we cannot physically touch now we can go one better. We can be as one, so remember this in good times and bad times for everyone has these. I can not only be by your side, but I can be you as you can be me and, together, we will do wonders and have that which was so special in our lives on earth.

That's all for the moment my darling; remember these words for I love you; I am you and you are me.

Joan

22 September 2017

Hello, my precious

I love you just as I used to when I was in the physical body, but now in a different and all-encompassing way. I am in the privileged position of knowing our previous lives and our life plans for my recent and your current incarnation on earth.

I cannot divulge too much, but we have been together for eons and, as such, there is a magnetic pull between us. The love between our souls is as one and as pure as can be: like a stream making its way from the peaks of the Himalayas and becoming stronger and stronger as it completes its journey to the sea. Nothing will change its power and direction, for its will and purpose is of the Creator. Such is our love my darling and, as you take time to assess your life in the days and weeks ahead, open yourself to me and God as you commence the most important period of your life.

You find it incredible that you can go into the silence and then speak wonderful words of wisdom. You have been prepared for this over a very long time; so, be ready for anything. You work and play extremely hard and have taken on worldly responsibilities of a caring nature. Be open to possible changes, which will just happen without any difficulty. Everything will fit together like a jigsaw as you specialise in one direction on the spiritual pathway. Do not worry; you will take it in your stride and, together, we will complete the special mission that your life will become.

Take care of yourself. Enjoy every moment of your life; eat and sleep well and you will walk with the Great Spirit to fulfil the climax of your life's purpose. May God be ever by your side, guiding and protecting you with His love, and be ever mindful of my presence as we become as one again in spirit.

With eternal love.

Joan

***

5 April 2016

Someone has been trying to get in to speak to you and has, indeed, been sharing a few minutes with you while you have been occupied with important thoughts of your Creator. She remembers well your discussions, especially the ones referring to 'nobody being here', (laughter). So, if you like, she will start from that viewpoint.

> Joan:
> You have all been thinking of me at this time (her birthday) and your love has reached me, has touched me beyond measure, for whilst I continually think of you, all of you, I cannot expect the same in return. Those few words seem to be opposite to the meaning of nobody being here, but we do know the real meaning for we discussed it so many times, (laughter). We also discussed the words, 'there is only One', and I can see the meaning more clearly now that I am on this side of life. Nevertheless, I appreciate, like I did on earth, that you have your own individual lives to lead but, when you can think and be aware of all life as One, your individual life will be more than you would expect for the mere fact of *feeling* at One with others brings new life to your body, to your whole being.
>
> It starts within at the heart centre and spreads throughout the body but, above all, it has a calming and healing effect on the mind. The mind all too often is led away into different corners, into worries, sometimes into sad thoughts, but when you go beyond yourself then you are changing your mindset completely. You are looking upwards and outwards with love and your whole presence feels inspired. So, do take time to be as One.
>
> I am still very busy, as you would expect, but I do have time to keep my eye on a few of you. I am sorry when any of you are not well and I try to help all of you. When you think of me I am sure you think of fun and laughter, and the work that we did together. The enjoyment we had when serving, when helping in different

ways, when simply doing some cooking, when being there for others. Well, I am always there for you not in the physical but, if anything, more importantly in spirit.

So, I return all the love you have given me over the past day or so and say how pleased I am that you are still meeting together, that you still have this wonderful relationship. I am trying my best to get into that head of his (the Channel's) – he won't mind me saying it – to prompt the memory of the times we spent together when we both had such amazing spiritual experiences, not only in India but in England as well. I am aware, now that I am here, of all the things you have done that I was not aware of and I am so pleased and know that those you helped are truly grateful. Some may not be aware of it but I am.

I feel at this moment as though the clock has been turned back and that we are all in a lively mood, laughing as we discussed books and teachings, in particular one by Nisargadatta. I did have trouble with that one, (laughter) and I know that occasionally one or two of you look at his book, or writings, and you, speaking the words, (Channel) even looked this morning and put it down quickly! We enjoyed it, even though we may not have understood much of it, (laughter).

The teachings that we ask you to channel, some of which have been put into the book and some which will go into the next one, are presented more clearly and are more easily read by people in the Western world. We have much work to do together and I know that, with your goodwill and love, and my help and all those here who are so willing to be part of what is to be done, will make for a very happy time; just like the old times when we were together. You only have to think of those times and I am there sharing them with you.

3 January 2016

Before we leave you, there is someone who wishes to say a few words. I am sure you are guessing who is coming to the fore now.

Joan:
I bring my love to you all.

Time is going on since I was on the earth plane: time for you that is because, for me, there is no time and yet there is something which shows that we have been apart physically for some time. But that does not make any difference. If anything, it improves our relationship; my relationship with all of you. We joke about things, and isn't it good to laugh, but the serious note is we have never really been apart, just one body different from another, one vibration different from another.

You ask what we did for Christmas, or what we do for Christmas. Most of us spend some of our time with you, for where else and what else would we want to do? We want to be with our families, our friends, to share in their joy in their happy times but, as you know, we all have different lives to live over here so we carry on with what we are doing, what we have to do, what we want to do, what we do on our pathways, for there is never a time when one does not have a pathway.

We do have celebrations, we have concerts, we get together and party in a different way and we have festivals and there is one, of course, about this time of your year. Very difficult to compare time when it doesn't exist, with time on your planet where it does exist. We still meet and have celebrations, but we always pay homage to the Great Spirit, to the Creator of all life, for we all are on the main pathway returning to that wonderful, wonderful, unbelievable, incredible intelligence. Joy beyond thought, abundance beyond thought, happiness, perfect light and love; we all celebrate as we come closer to the Great Spirit.

Sitter:

Thank you, Joan. We miss you, but we feel close when you come and speak to us like this.

Joan:

It's my pleasure. I really love being with you but, unfortunately, time on your side runs out and I have to leave you, but with all my love and best wishes for a very happy and successful year. God bless you.

***

23 February 2016

This leads us on to the time when we occasionally ask if you have anything to say, anything to ask, or do you just wish to sit in the peace that is here at the moment? We know our Channel would like to ask a question; he queries:

> Q: *How can we give a message through a medium, describe ourselves and, yet, at another time appear to be someone with great knowledge from spirit coming through to give teachings? The two don't seem to marry up.*

A: There are several reasons for this. One is that we like to come back to people and show, through mediums, how we looked, how we felt, our mannerisms and things that only you would know. When we come to our side of life a great vista opens up to us when we are ready. We have everything before us, we have all the knowledge that we need, all we ask for. We become different in our outlook, for we experience in a totally different way.

We have left behind our bodies. We can fly, we can do what we like and we have available to us the knowledge we have gained on earth with our various lives, and also the knowledge we have gained over here. When the situation calls for it we can be that same one just described, or we can appear to be a very knowledgeable teacher, and this has happened several times to our Channel here. There is nothing strange about it, nothing that you would not really expect if you lived here, for we have so much available to us on our side of life. We have tremendous opportunities and many, many of us wish to help people on the earth in different ways.

So, we can one day be a great teacher and another day appear as we were on the earth. We hope that has been of interest and help.

21 March 2017

Happiness is so evident here today. We wonder if you wish to say anything, or ask any questions, or just dwell in happiness? It is up to you. If you do not have any questions, we have a question for you.

> Q: *What makes you take decisions in your life that you sometimes regret, and at other times you are so pleased that you wonder who made those decisions?*

> A: Sitter: When I, personally, make a decision it's the right decision at the time. As time goes on it can prove to be the wrong decision but it was the right decision at the time, and you learn from that. Each wrong thing you have done you learn from it; the right decisions work out even better. That's my answer.

It's a wonderful answer because everyone is on the earth to experience. So, if mistakes are made and the wrong decisions taken then that person will experience in a different way: but then you will ask, Was I meant to take that decision? The answer to that is if you needed the experience then that was the right decision for you. There is also an element of freedom: you must feel free, you must feel the decision is yours. As this life has such a wide perspective you can indulge yourselves in things you thought perhaps you shouldn't because you will then know that in the future you needn't go down that route again.

You are also here to express yourselves, to enjoy yourselves, to go beyond what you were expected to do and when you have gone beyond an important goal that will help you so much in your future. It will save you time in other lives and bring you the happiness that you deserve. There is also another thought: when you come across people you imagine were taking the wrong decisions, creating havoc and, worse still, causing wars, have they done it because it was in their plan? Have they done it because they were foolish?

In other words, someone who comes to the earth and does what you would suggest is an evil thing, that person may be an advanced soul and he has been given the task so that other people may have experiences they need. This is a very deep subject and we don't want to say too much about that today other than please don't judge, for you may be judging for the wrong reasons and, when you judge and criticise in a bad way, these vibrations can come back to you.

So, we say to you, when you are on the earth, do take the decisions you need to. Do ask for help both from your Creator and from us but you, yourselves, must take decisions as they feel right to you. When you have taken the right decision you will know and, as our friend said, what appear to be wrong decisions can later turn out to be the right ones, for you, and others, would have experienced as you were meant to.

Well, I don't know where this is leading us but, before we close, if there is anything else anyone wishes to say please do so, for this circle is a two-way connection. We may be giving most of the words but we appreciate the words and thoughts from you as well. In fact, one day I think we will set aside time so that we can bring forward a subject for debate.

27 June 2017

Q: *I found that learning to forgive people for what they said when I was young has been a really difficult mountain for me to climb.*

A: That is one of the biggest reasons you're here. You all have many reasons why you have come to the earth.

Q: *You think you have forgiven people but it still rankles at the back of your mind. So, is that forgiveness or refusing to forget?*

A: What's the famous phrase, 'I'll forgive them, but not forget'. That's not forgiveness, is it? Pure forgiveness forgets.

11 July 2017

Q: *Regarding your talk on the adverse effect on the planet of today's IT communications, satellites and the like, I don't see how I can send out. What do I send out, apart from love, to prevent all this stuff that's killing the world?*

A: Please excuse our laughter. There *is* only love so you have hit the nail on the head. Therefore, in one way, when you send out love it covers that as well.

Q: *I wondered if visualisation, gathering it all up and throwing it away, might help?*

A: Just a little thought in that direction is sufficient. You know more than we do!

25 July 2017

Q: *I think everybody has a different nature, but why are people miserable? I don't understand, because I am what I am. I can't understand the misery that people put upon themselves.*

A: Yes, it's more than just what appears on the surface. People have lived many lives and they bring back the totality of those lives. Therefore, if they created misery to others in their previous lives then they are going to have misery in a next life. That is only part of it: sometimes people elect to come to the earth in a negative state and their journey may take them from this state into a positive state to get out of their misery.

There are many reasons for this. We can understand because having been a human being it is natural to live the life one feels inside and when one cannot live that life, due to circumstances, one can become very miserable. Also, one can explode within and go on a life that experiences the depths. We could tell you what some of your lives have been like but we don't feel it would serve a purpose at the moment. However, all people, all souls, who have lived on the earth at some time or another have experienced miserable times as well as happy times. It is a matter of progress and I am sure you have seen that some people have sunk to the depths before they can start climbing and reaching the heights again.

Sometimes, it seems one came to the earth on a fairly level key and, therefore, did not have to experience the depths, but most people do have difficult experiences from which they can learn. It is how one deals with those experiences that helps to form their overall character. I understand you may not comprehend why other people are so miserable but be pleased you do not have that misery in you.

Q: *That makes sense, thank you. Then, again, why do people commit murder and does it all come down to character and how they are?*

Everybody is so different and that is what you were saying, that it's a learned lesson to take with you into the next life.

A: You asked why people commit murder. There are many answers to that: karma – some people ridicule it – but cause and effect does take place.

Q: *Yes, I understand cause and effect, but I hadn't thought of it in that respect with murder. That's a good thought.*

A: It doesn't mean that if you murder someone in this lifetime then that person will murder you in the next life but it has happened and it could, say, after five lifetimes. There are also mitigating circumstances in situations when a murder wasn't meant to take place. It is very difficult for us to explain but the Great Spirit, the overall intelligence behind all life, can arrange it so that people learn a great deal. It sounds harsh, but only if you see the whole picture of previous and future lives can you appreciate why this happens.

Q: *A hard lesson is going to be very hard to learn, isn't it?*

A: Yes, but I can assure you that the lessons one is given to learn on the earth cannot be greater than one is able to take. So, when you feel sorry for someone who is going through a very bad patch remember there is more to it than appears.

Q: *Yes, it is hard to think of that, isn't it?*

A: Yes, it is. In your lives it is very difficult to appreciate it all. When you come to our side of life you will see so much more; you will appreciate why things happened.

24 February 2015

Has anyone any questions or anything to say or any words they may wish to impart? Now is the time.

Q: I'd like to ask a question and it's with regard to Masters. Are there always the same number of Masters in the spirit world, or does it vary?

A: Thank you. I don't know where that question came from (laughter). Masters or so-called Masters are everywhere. They are, even now, on the earth plane as well as in spirit. A true Master can be in more places than one so, therefore, yes you could say there are always the same number of Masters in spirit, for they are in more places than one.

However, that is not strictly true because there are other Masters who spend their life on earth and become Christed. You do not always hear about these Masters for they often operate in small areas; they are not looking to be known throughout the world. They are able to become enlightened in their own way by giving up their normal lives. They open themselves completely, one hundred per cent, to the Spirit, to the Godhead, and they become Masters.

What is the meaning of the word Master? On earth it is that they have mastered their thoughts, their words, their feelings, their desires, so much so that they are not led into areas they do not wish to go. They do not do things that they wished they had not. They do not have harsh words for people that are not meant. They may act as though they are telling people off but the intention is not to hurt in any way, just to educate and help people, so they are mastering their life on earth. To master everything within one, to you and people like you, must seem quite incredible because you have all experienced doing things that you have regretted. So, can you imagine having complete control over your every action, word and thought?

That is the meaning of mastering life on earth. You are all on the road to mastery. So, to answer your question, although it may appear that there are no additional Masters in spirit, as each one becomes close to the Great Spirit and eventually merges with Him, it would seem there would be one less Master but it does not work like that. You may have heard of Avatars who are direct incarnations of God and can take a life on earth at any time, having already merged with the Great Spirit.

As you are beginning to gather you have asked a very complicated question, or should I say the answer is very complicated. It is really made complicated for your minds because of the intricacies of spirit. As you progress further you don't appear as an individual so, as you become One, there are no numbers any more but, as we have just explained, you can still come to earth as a full Master. You can also spend time on earth at the same time as being in spirit, but then you would be in your spirit body which can be seen by people if it is desired by the Master.

We don't feel we have done justice to your question, but we hope that some of the information we have given is of help.

8 November 2016

Q: In our world we see the sun, the moon, all the planets and all the stars in the heavens: that's our world. What is the skyline like in your world, in spirit? Do you have the same one? I've read it's totally different: would you just give an overview, please?

A: Thank you for that important and interesting question.

First of all, let us say that what we see in spirit, i.e. our environment, depends so much on our previous lives and especially on our immediate past life, for we go to the appropriate place according to our understanding and the love that we have shown in our previous life. Taking a situation where a wonderful life has been spent serving others, and finding the truth of God within, then this person will go to an area that will feel natural to them.

At first it will seem like a dream for, as you said, on your earth you have the physical planets and the sky. Here, we have no need for that and, yet, we have so much more. We have a beautiful sky that envelops us all. It feels as though we are the sky; it feels as though we are the sun, for we do have our own sun, but it is not like your sun. It appears round and warm, not more heat or cold, just right, and all around we have beautiful flowers, trees, the like you haven't seen on earth.

We have wonderful buildings that are not real but seem so when one is in them. In a way, it is like being on earth but a million times better. We have no need for the planets and, yet, we still have the stars and we can travel between the stars because, by thought, we can be anywhere. Again, it is not like sitting on the earth looking up at the stars above you. They are all around us and, in a way, they are us and we are them. So, everything is linked but it is very difficult for us to explain to you with your earthly minds.

What we would say is that when you come to spirit this is the sort of experience you will have but there are greater and greater environments for those who have progressed further than us. There are, of course, very grey and dark environments for those souls who are on the bottom of the ladder. Even so, once the ones lower down really wish to progress, they will soon have a better life and a better environment.

The colours here are manifold; they, again, appear as though they are you and you are them. Life here is so beautiful and so rewarding but we still have the need to work, to serve, for there are many on our side who need help and we come to help you on your side of life. We do all this within the feeling and enjoyment of where we live. We hope that gives you a little indication of what life is like over here.

12 January 2016

Yes, it is that time again when we ask if you have anything to say; to comment on what has been said or, indeed, to ask us anything. We leave it up to you, dear friends.

> Q: *I have a question I've been wanting to ask. We've been reading a book recently which states that each planet is controlled by a spirit, just as the Christ Spirit controls this world. So, does the Ether spirit control the ether planets in this universe? Could you comment on any of it, please?*

A: Thank you. As usual you do not make life easy for us with your questions, (laughter).

It is well-known that each planet and, indeed, each star, each heavenly body is spirit as well as physical. The planets you refer to, I believe, are in the solar system, is that correct?

Q: *Yes.*

A: What is little-known, of course, is that there is actually life on all the planets, but not in the way of the earth. It is true there is an overriding spirit force that is not in charge but is the caretaker of each planet for each planet and each star would not exist without the spirit part of it. As you are spirit within a physical body so with the planets but, as you understand, it goes further than that for the spirit is within each atom and there is nowhere that does not contain spirit. If you want, you can put names to these spirits that are the guardians of each planet, but I don't think it is necessary at this stage.

You may have heard people say, 'as above so below', 'as below so above'. In other words, wherever you are the same principle is there. As in the heavens, so in the planets. All life looks different on each planet but each one contains the God Spirit. All planets and all stars contain the Guardian spirit which is at One with the overriding Great Spirit and part of their job is to ensure that all planets move according to their destiny; the same with stars. You are able to see distant stars, new stars and also old stars called black holes, so there is a pattern in all life especially in the universe.

We agree with what you have been reading that, yes, there is spirit on each planet, but more than that, there are individual spirits all being connected as you are on earth.

***

5 April 2016

We said at the beginning that this circle would be different today. What we would like to do in a moment is for you to think on two words that you often see and hear and write. They are 'I AM'. Think on these words, be inspired and put down your thoughts. If they are channelled, so be it; if they are what appear to be your own conscious thoughts, that is fine.

Take a few moments to open up, absorb the sound of these words in your mind, the meaning and what they can do for you and others.

Thoughts On I AM By Circle Members

Sitter 1:
Emptiness, where everything is.

Sitter 2:
I AM in you and you are in Me; no separation.
I AM all that there is and ever will be.
Every particle, every atom is filled by Me.
I AM the Provider and Giver; my love is the same for all.
I AM that which you seek, within and without.
Everything is contained within Me and you, if you did but realise it.
Trust in the I AM.
Live in the I AM.
Love in the I AM.
For I AM.

Sitter 3:
I AM the basis of all life, the indefinable Great Spirit from whom all life comes and into whom all life returns.

Simply by saying these words silently or out loud they will have the same effect as chanting the OM, the original sound.

Meditate on these words and they will take you within to the special place in your heart where, it is said, God resides.

This helps you in silence to feel the expansion of this area until your whole body is flooded with bliss.

It is from here that you are in touch with all life and you will be inspired to fulfil your life's plan.

May your life be forever filled with the One Great Spirit!

Chapter Three

On the Pathway

The clock is ticking: the clock of your earthly lives. How long have you left on earth? Will you come to us tomorrow, or will you come in fifty, sixty, seventy years? You don't know; we have an idea but we cannot tell you. As the days go by, as the clock keeps ticking, do you wonder what you have still to do? Do you think you are doing all you can, or are you feeling that you have done enough?

We would say to you that your life counts right up until the last second you live on earth. Be in touch with your Father God, for in that way you will know what your next move is to be. There are pressures in your world; there are pressures when you are working and, today, employers want more and more from you.

Some people who are retired may appear to have a full day, but is this time being spent in the most beneficial way? Only they know this. However, you all know within what you have come for. You may not know in the mind but, within you, it is written, your whole life plan is written. So, do keep in touch with your inner self.

When there are pressures, when life seems too busy, then so much is missed in life. There is sufficient time to do everything you want, everything you have come for, but it means that you have to open yourself, give of yourself, and be in touch with your real self, your spirit. You will then have all the time you need.

Isn't it extraordinary how people show their greed after Christmas? I'm referring to what used to be called the January sales, but now they start the day after Christmas although preparations for them must have started before Christmas. You have scenes of people queueing and even fighting over items that appear to be very good bargains. Not content with spending the first day at the sales, some return day after day as though their lives depended upon it.

Your papers announce that the retail trade is suffering because of the weather, or other reasons, as they are geared up to selling frantically before Christmas and in the sales thereafter. It was a tradition to have January sales; then they became earlier and earlier and now some shops even change their displays before the end of Christmas Eve. What is the cause of this state of affairs; is it the shops who want to cash in on people's greed and expectations, or is it the people themselves, for without customers the shops would not open?

It is symptomatic in this age on your earth that people want something for nothing, or a bargain. It doesn't seem a question of whether there is a need for what people buy in these sales. That word need seems to be forgotten by the masses, who clamour in the shops day after day to have the latest this or that. Contrast this with people who can't even afford the fare to the shops, let alone the cost of the goods. They are just scraping a living and their shopping is comprised only of food and the occasional piece of necessary clothing.

How has this all developed? It seems to be because people have forgotten, or are unaware of, who they really are. They have forgotten who provides all their food, clothing and the latest gadgetry. Yes, very little thought is generally given to who provides everything to enable life on your planet to exist. When one takes time to go within, to talk and pray to the Creator, one begins to see life in a different light.

One will be so grateful for this life on earth, to find peace beyond understanding that is always there within each and every person on your planet. A remarkable change begins to occur within, with one's attitude, from wanting to giving. A realisation takes place that everything belongs to God and you are all on the earth as guardians and caretakers of the land and buildings you call home.

If nothing is yours, why are you queueing up to buy so frenziedly the so-called bargains in your shops? Once the loving realisation occurs that all is God and all *is* God's, the greed and a must have attitude for the latest sale offerings gradually disappears, being replaced by a wonderful satisfaction and gratefulness to God for what you already have. The continued wanting is gradually replaced by a feeling of giving, giving of oneself, to those you know and those you have yet to meet, whether it be monetary, physical items or giving of love expressed in terms of time and care for others.

A life spent in giving, rather than wanting, results in something you cannot buy. It is the wonder of feeling your God within you, feeling at peace with yourself, happiness not known before, excitement within and appreciation for the smallest sights of nature, for the beautiful smile of a baby and the love that is seen in response to giving.

Who, therefore, is the happier; the one wanting or the one giving?

New Year is the time when people have rested and they are preparing to resume normal activities.

What is normal? Normal is described as a state to which people become accustomed, but what seems normal for one can appear abnormal to another. Each person is unique in that they not only vibrate differently, they have different levels of satisfaction, different pain levels and so on. In fact, whatever you name, is experienced by each person in a different way.

It is good to remember this, for on earth it is so easy to judge another: but what one is judging may not be the same experience for the person being judged. In other words, you are not all on a level playing field and to judge another means that you think you are in that person's shoes. Then you judge in the way that you would react to certain circumstances, whereas the person you are judging has a different perception.

There are many reasons why one shouldn't judge, but it is all too easy to do so. We know, we have been there and we have all judged and taken the consequences. However, once you get to the stage of becoming non-judgemental you begin to see that, although different, all is still One, all is connected.

God created a multiplicity of species, and different races of humans, according to environment. Now, of course, with communications so advanced, with air travel and with countries receiving not only refugees but others wishing to emigrate, the original native population of a particular country may be much in decline. This brings with it many challenges, but also gives growth opportunities for, just as you have the potential to meet people from different races, from different backgrounds and with different values, then the impulse to judge is that much greater. The secret is to overcome judgment and one can do this by remembering that God created all as One. You do not have to like the personalities of certain people, but you can love what they stand for; you can love the spirit within.

Returning to the time of year when business starts again and people are looking to the future – some making New Year resolutions, others who don't bother because they always break them – one can assess where one is on this adventure of life on earth. Yes, it is an adventure if one looks positively at it. When problems arise, they can be met with an active mind, ready to resolve whatever problem exists and move on, for nothing remains the same.

There is change all around you; always change. For instance, your weather is changing. People call it global warming, but it is more than that. It comes back to the natural law of action and reaction and what humans have done to the planet, resulting in changing weather patterns. There are so many ways in which reactions can happen. If one is aware of this then one has a greater understanding, and it is yet another reason not to judge.

Looking back at your lives, and assessing where you are, do you have that peaceful feeling within? When you feel in a peaceful state at all times, then you are well-set for the rest of your lives.

Your thoughts may sometimes turn to reincarnation and why, if there is such a thing, one doesn't remember previous lives.
In our experience there is reincarnation. It is not quite as you probably imagine, but you have, in some form or another, lived many, many, earthly lives and those experiences help to mould one's thoughts, attitude and character. What you call your personality is derived from them.

First of all, if you are in the moment then it doesn't matter. Most people have times in their lives when they have memories or feelings of being somewhere that they haven't physically visited before. They may also have been given messages that they were in a particular place in a previous life.

If you could see your own lives, you would see a pattern which covers the whole spectrum: rich lives, poor lives, the hard ones and the easy ones. You would then understand what your current life is about. It is, therefore, much better that you have no recollection of your previous lives when you are born, for otherwise that would tend to hold you back from certain experiences in the current incarnation.

However, the philosophy of reincarnation is a good subject to discuss. Whether you are experiencing good times or bad times in the body, as you progress spiritually your thoughts are bound to turn to the continuity of life and whether you have been on the earth before. Suffice it to say that life goes on and on into infinity. The soul learns a great deal on the earth but cannot learn everything in one lifetime, and so it seems sensible that the soul will have more than one incarnation.

We realise this is a complex subject and, as you have come to understand when going deeply into the spiritual philosophy of Oneness, when you reach a certain stage there is no need for future lives on earth. That doesn't mean to say that they haven't happened, or won't happen, just that the understanding is there that they may not be necessary any more. When you go further in realising that all is One, where the individual is no longer paramount, there is no need to think of past or future lives. Nevertheless, as you are on the earth for a purpose it is good to take advantage of living that life to the full.

We return to the thought and the message to be always in the moment, for being in the moment allows you to experience fully all that is around you, all that is within you. As you become closer to your God and feel part of Him, beginning to feel He is in you and you are in Him, then all these other thoughts do not matter. When you are in that state it is more than bliss, more than awareness, it is more than happiness, it just *is*. It is *beingness,* and when you are in this state nothing matters. Everything, whether you are experiencing what you call good or bad, is taken in a state of equilibrium.

So, to be always in the moment is the ideal for you on earth, and this is all very well until the mind comes in and raises many questions. When you can be in the moment, even when you are busy doing things, you will find that your lives change and go forward with a feeling of satisfaction that you are travelling along your chosen pathway for this lifetime.

In your world today non-violence is not a way that the leaders of the world seem to choose: rather, they prefer to stockpile more armaments to protect their own country. We are at the stage, once again, when more and more nuclear heads have been manufactured than would be needed to remove several planets, not just one small country.

Therefore, to speak of non-violence having regard to armaments in the world today, at first seems rather ridiculous. However, what does non-violence mean? Normally it means not hurting anyone, not attacking; but you know it means much more. Non-violence is at the heart of everyone, for their very thoughts are either non-violent or violent.

To have peace in one's mind would be thought of as non-violent but wanting peace at the same time as putting conditions on it is not peace at all. So, non-violence with conditions is not non-violence either. Non-violence is a form of love, for pure unconditional love has no harmful thoughts whatsoever. Unconditional love has a massive meaning and it is more than caring for and liking somebody. It is really a state of mind and so is non-violence.

Non-violence can be part of one's make-up and you see people every day who don't have a hurtful thought in them, even when they are provoked. It takes courage to be non-violent under provocation, but that is what is required in the world today.

To be totally non-violent throughout one's life is almost impossible. Look back at the times when you have been angry. It happens in everyone's life, but when one can learn from past feelings to when one just gives loving non-violent thoughts, one is better prepared for the next time there is provocation. It becomes, as we have said, a state of mind, a state within one where the possibility of violence does not exist.

This leads to overcoming all thoughts of violence, all thoughts of unkind action against another. So, the true path of non-violence can be taken to the extreme and a person who acts solely in that way is permanently protected from violence. If any of the world leaders would completely turn around the politics of ploughing more and more money into armaments for the security of their countries, then they could spend the money on the education of non-violence. The natural law of love would then overcome any problem, providing that love is entirely unconditional.

We say again, that to practice non-violence and preach peace must be wholly unconditional. To have non-violence in your nature, and thus live it, one becomes an example showing that non-violence is the answer to man's problems.

When people first arrive in the spirit world, especially if they have followed an orthodox religion, they tend to look for the same. After realising they are not dead after all, they think everything in their lives will be the same and it takes some souls a long time to adjust. They are, of course, in for a surprise because the beauty, everything on our side of life, is accentuated manifold. Many cannot believe it, for they were expecting either heaven or hell and so a lot were very pleased to find themselves in the former!

As you know, there is no hell. It comes from within an individual, whether on your side of life, or on our side of life. If someone is a troubled soul when they reach us things don't change immediately. They usually spend, in your time, many weeks, months or years becoming adjusted to life over here. For these people help is needed and help is given. They still feel within the troubles they brought with them, but the opportunity is given to learn the truth. Gradually, with help, most souls begin to relish life over here.

Now, for the average person, once they get over the initial shock they, too, start to enjoy life and they will see such treasures, such beauty, as they could never have imagined.

All souls assess their previous life when they are ready: comparable to seeing a video or DVD on the earth. While parts can be very troublesome, there will also have been happy times in their lives and they will enjoy reliving these. The review is arranged so that they can cope with the difficult periods; they are encouraged, by friends and angels, to look forward rather than backward. As they become adjusted to their new life, they will want to rectify actions that they now regret. They will be given opportunities and they will be able to serve, for now they will probably have a desire to do so.

All people who come to our side of life, even those you think would have led an almost perfect life, will have some skeletons in the cupboard. So, all people may feel a little uncomfortable when reviewing their lives, but they will be astounded to see how their various actions have affected others.

Most people will have a certain portion of their lives to be proud of and we rejoice with them as they see the result of their good works. Others, who are not so fortunate, are encouraged and helped and they, too, will be given opportunities on this side of life to serve, both here and on the earth.

As most souls become adjusted to their new way of life, they will still live with the thoughts of their previous life on earth. As we have mentioned, they can still go to church and keep their old beliefs but, gradually, they will come to understand the truth.

We cannot emphasise enough that the opportunities here are so great. The beauty is outstanding, not just in the landscape but in all aspects of our life. We have feelings, just as you, and when we are in the presence of the Masters we, too, have the bliss that we know you have all felt at some time or other. There are no limits here; all have equal opportunities and life can be as exciting and wonderful as one wishes to make it.

So, we come back to thinking of you on the earth plane. Most people are frightened of death and do not want to leave. They will do anything to extend their lives on earth, but when they arrive on our side of life they will wonder what they were worried about, for life here is absolutely incredible.

What is a friend? Who is a friend? Can one be a friend to all? Someone once described strangers as friends she hadn't yet met. What a wonderful attitude, a positive attitude, assuming the best in people rather than the worst. She was looking for the *real* person within, for the best friend one can ever have is God Himself. God, we understand, likes to be a friend to people, not set in an ivory tower, unapproachable, directing the universe. No! Our loving God is within life, is a friend to everyone, is *waiting* to be a friend to everyone.

Take a moment to think about who your real friends are. What do you do to become friends, or what do you omit to do? Do you open yourselves, being honest with everyone, or do you hold something back, keeping something in reserve, not letting people know the real you? If only everyone was completely open and honest with each other, so that anything could be said without causing offence, then the world would already be paradise but, unfortunately, that is not the case on your earth today.

Most people are lucky to have more real friends than the number of fingers on one hand. Why are people afraid of being completely open in front of so-called friends and acquaintances? It seems that they are either frightened of becoming too involved or frightened of letting other people into their most inner sanctuary, the private place within.

It is by doing just that, by letting others into your most private inner being, your thought centre, your pure real self which is spirit, that you open your real self to others and create a link with their inner selves, their real selves. You will then feel a true connection, unconditional love, not attachment, not worrying about a commitment, but unconditional love which overrides all worries, façades, and thus becomes the basis for real friendship.

In this way you become a true friend. You get to know people better and, of course, you become a friend to your God who dwells in the sacred place within.

We wish to say a few words about life on earth, as we see it, for most of us feel privileged to have lived on your earth many times. We have memories and can see how those lives were connected, how there was a reason for each life following the other. There may have been hundreds of years between them, but there is a connection each time one manifests on earth.

A further reason, not known when you are on earth, is that you and all people who incarnate are, in fact, playing a part like actors on a stage. It doesn't feel like it when you are in the middle of problems, or arguments but, believe us, you are playing a part. You agreed before you came to the earth what type of life you would have, where you would live, where you would go, and many, many, other actions that take place in your life. If you look back you can see a pattern in it; so, imagine that from our perspective we can see a much bigger picture overall.

Remember, especially when times are difficult, that you are playing a part. You may be sad or joyful, and we are sure you would be playing your part very well at that time, but remember a good actor plays his part and then gets on with his own life. He does not live the part he is playing in the theatre for the rest of his life. So, if you look upon your lives as playing your part then you will have a different view of your life on earth.

However, it is not as simple as that, as you might imagine. Fortunately, by the way you live, and the way you play your part, you can make your lives brighter and enjoy your time on earth so much more than you expected. It depends upon your attitude, upon your love for humankind and, indeed, for the animals, the birds, and all life. When you have an outgoing personality, showing love for all life, you will not suffer pain as much as you may have done otherwise, for there is something in the cells of your bodies which reacts with the love you send out.

Have you noticed that people with many, many, problems just continue having problems for the rest of their lives? They talk about it, they grumble, they complain and, therefore, this has an effect on their bodies. Conversely, when they are happy, when they are optimistic, when they are enjoying life and providing fun and help for others, then their bodies will receive a boost so that, when the time comes for them to experience problems, these will not be as great as they could have been.

So, while you are playing your parts you still have the opportunity to live a wonderful life, a happy life, a life that you will be proud of when it comes to an end.

Easter Sunday is a very famous festival on your earth and a time of joy. We perceive the good vibrations and say that when there is joy around the earth its aura shines more brightly. The earth itself is a living being, as you know, and is affected by all life making it their home. Just as in a family when the children are arguing and being unpleasant then the conditions are not good for harmony and growth. So, too, the earth.

The earth is affected by what takes place all around its surface and, indeed, under the surface as man continually searches for new metals and energies. If you could see the earth, the structure, the crust, and below, you would know that there is continual movement, for the earth, like all living beings, is continually evolving. If there was not movement and evolvement things would slow down and eventually stop; so, we must expect movement throughout the earth. You see it on top of the earth with all vegetation, how it comes to life and dies back and, too, below the surface. It is like the blood that keeps the body warm, at the right temperature, and through the various constituents in the blood which keep the body moving properly.

We started to say that the earth can be affected by what is happening with people and with the conditions all around. It needs bright times, joyful times, to keep it going in a peaceful and satisfactory manner. You only normally see the surface of the earth and although your scientists come up with ideas of what is within, including the very hot core of the earth, they cannot see the spiritual part which enables its life to continue.

It is the spirit which keeps nature active and revolving and makes the earth appear so beautiful when looked upon from space and, indeed, when viewed by the naked eye to see the beautiful flowers, the trees, the magnificent trees. It needs the Great Spirit to keep it functioning as it should but, also, when people are happy then the earth can move forward more freely in its planned evolution.

We see more happiness for parts of the earth at this festive season. Unfortunately, the members of your governments and their workers have lost the ability to be quiet and be at One with their God. In so many cases they have no religion, nor any spiritual convictions and they think everything has happened by chance. We, here, know how wrong that is for there is purpose to all life; the secret is to move with that natural life, to evolve in the way that the Great Spirit designed it. Your animals, your birds, indeed the trees and the flowers, are automatically at One with nature, or spirit. It is only when man changes the way that animals live by moving them around, by using scientific experiments on them, that leaves the animal kingdom sometimes going in a different direction to what was originally intended for them.

Now, we come to mankind where such a fantastic opportunity for living at One has been lost for so many centuries and even millennia. When man returns to his original state within then he will be happy; he will be fulfilled, he will not be bored. He will always have an aim in life; even when that life is coming to an end he will know its purpose and he will be ready when it is his turn to move to our world. In-between he will have a myriad of opportunities of love, of contentment, of satisfying his enquiring mind, of living together peacefully and, yet, still having an exciting life, a life that is forever unique to him, a life of adventure coupled with love, peace and joy.

You may think this is utopia, and indeed it is, for it is only man himself that prevents this perfect life. You have your own heaven within so think along these lines, especially if you have problems or there are misunderstandings, for nothing in this life runs smoothly for ever. Only when the earth returns, together with its people, to its natural state will this happen.

We come to you as ever, and bring love, healing and joy.

We sometimes go deeply into life on our side of the divide, but the most important thing is that you, and the people on earth, live your lives in the way predestined before you took this incarnation.

We are here to help those on the earth plane who need more information, who may have drifted from their chosen path, those with many problems at this time and those who are open and looking for communication from us. You offer yourselves, not necessarily by word, but by your attitude, your application and your love for all mankind.

As you go through life you meet more people and learn of others who are in need. It seems on your earth today that there are more problems than ever but, as we have said before, you make your own problems. You come to the earth with a blueprint and know beforehand the type of situations that will cause difficulties and stretch you in one way or another. You also know that you will be given help to meet these challenges, just as you help others to deal with their challenges. It is so reassuring for someone to have friends on the end of a phone, friends who will drop everything and come at a moment's notice if it is necessary.

The problems you read about can really trouble some people, but with understanding you come to realise that, in the totality of existence, a lifetime is only of short duration, for there is no death and life continues in one form or another throughout the ages. Have you ever taken that in; the thought that you have been here and other places for what you would describe as eons? It does not seem possible, but you are part of the Great Spirit and the Spirit essence within you, within every cell, has existed for all time. You all have tremendous histories locked away somewhere in that special place.

Have you ever thought, where did that come from? Where did that knowledge, that piece of advice, come from? It is all stored away and when you reach the stage of having your own key to open the secrets of your soul you will be amazed. You will find life even more enchanting, even more exciting and even more beautiful, for you will have senses like those on our side of life. You will see things from a different perspective; you will see things as one hundred times more beautiful than you do now.

How do you get the key to unlock your soul? It would be easy for us to say give up the self, the physical self, the little self, but we realise that you cannot just say, 'I give up the little self', for in the next moment in life you will be challenged. Then you will realise how important that little self is to you.

No, we are saying live with *love*, live with and by love in everything you do, in the way you receive, in the way you give, in the way you examine things, in the way you talk to people, in the way you answer awkward questions. If you give love to everyone, from the smallest baby to the oldest person, if you can be alike to all people and not be affected by some with their rudeness, their brusqueness, then you are well on the way to finding the key you need. Although it is said you have to rid yourselves of the little self this is best done by living your life for others.

There is only love, the basis of all life; if you give unconditional love in everything you do you will become that love. You will become the purest version of love and then you will have that key. It is a challenge, but it *is* possible that you could achieve the key for yourself in this life, rather than waiting until you go to the other side.

There is a time and place for words, yet communication, on whatever level, does not have to be by word alone. It can be by thought and, more importantly, just *is*. It can be a feeling within, a feeling throughout the body, a tingling, an activity of the cells. You can be with someone sitting together and not a word is said and, yet, there is communication, Oneness, a joining together inwardly of two souls.

When you experience too many words in a communication, and feel frustrated when someone is talking nonstop without really saying anything of importance, it often results in you switching off your mind and not paying much attention. You also have the other extreme where too little is said, and in-between there are many variations.

You have other forms of communication, such as showing pleasure with a beautiful smile and, conversely, by showing unhappiness with a sad look. When you think about it you are always communicating in one form or another. By sitting still and thinking you can be communicating with your higher self, or with someone many miles away, for thoughts can be picked up over long distances. It may not be as though you are talking to one another but the essence of the thought can be received by the person you are thinking about.

So, never think you are totally alone. Not only do you have your thoughts, your memories, your ambitions, you also have your guides and loved ones in spirit who may be listening and waiting to be of service to you. Above all, you have your Creator within who hears and sees everything as He is omnipresent and within all life. When you pray to Him it is not as though you are praying to a distant figure; you are praying to your higher self.

Therefore, the opportunity you all have in communication is awesome, and when it is realised from within you will never feel alone again. It can be the most wonderful experience to sit in peace, love and silence and can lead to the pinnacle of Oneness with all life.

We think of you as being the same as us, except you are encased in a human body. This is restrictive, yet challenging, because you have opportunities on the earth that we do not have in spirit. It is wonderful when you realise what opportunities lie ahead for you. You felt this way before you came to the earth but, due to the memory of your previous life being wiped away for this incarnation, you may well look at things differently now.

Think back to when you were a child, when everything was new to you. You may not remember being a baby, but you were intrigued with everything at that time. Gradually, through sight and touch, you became more aware of what was around you. In time, as you learnt to walk and run, you showed a keenness and springlike attitude, enjoying every moment of the day especially as you experienced, through vision and hearing, new adventures.

So, take time to recall your feelings as a child when you were keen to try anything. Remember your enthusiasm and bring those feelings into your life today. You have not changed within; your soul and spirit are the same. Your mind and body age through time and one is supposed to become wiser, but however wise you are it would help to recollect being a child, for you still have that enthusiasm within when you find something new.

It is the same for those starting out on their spiritual life on earth. One is so keen to learn more, to listen to teachers of spirit, to read books containing ancient teachings and wisdom but, above all, to receive the grace of the Great Spirit within as you absorb your new-found teachings. Rest in them, meditate on them and note the feelings of love, peace and joy that envelop you as you become more aware of your Creator, who is within you and all life. You may have heard this many times, but until you experience it within it does not mean much to you.

People have always and will always be searching for truth, that truth which is within you all. There are different ways of continuing your search spiritually. Some people go on pilgrimages, travelling far and wide across the earth, often receiving great joy and wisdom, but it is not necessary, although helpful, to do this as you have the answers to all your questions within. Your spirit is linked to all life; it is the supreme God. So, be in touch with your spirit within and you will be in touch eternally with your Creator.

When He was on earth, Jesus told His followers that His love for them was that of the Father, the Father within all life, and to listen to the Lord's word in their innermost heart.

You can all hear the words of the Father within if you just be still and seek them. There is nothing that stops you other than yourself. So, be still and await the Lord's voice within you.

You have read the Word and you will hear the word within you. When will you step out in faith and believe you can do it? It is up to you and you alone.

Take that first step as a leap of faith and you will have it returned manifold. What are you waiting for?

Everything in the universe is balanced to perfection. So, too, is the human body, that incredible sheath which surrounds the soul and spirit in the individual. It was designed by the Creator to enable one to live and experience for a given period of time on the earth. Some people call it a miracle that the human body works so well, especially when it is young and fit and not abused by overeating, intoxication or social drug use. Even when it is abused it has extraordinary resilience and usually recovers in the course of time.

It is a fine instrument but only works with the grace of God, through His Spirit which is within all life. The spirit is within every atom and cell of the body and stays there from conception to the time of death, when your spirit and soul, containing the sum total of your recent life, returns to the spirit world. This can and will be seen when the soul has become settled in its new environment. Every single moment is recorded: one's fears, hopes, enjoyment, problems, reactions, love and caring for others, the list goes on. It should be something to look forward to, to relive all those happy moments. On the other side of the coin there are the unhappy moments, the unfriendly and possibly hurtful attitudes to people but, overall, most lives show an excess of positive traits.

The question is, would you make your life on earth different if you were aware of this information? Your soul was aware before you took birth, but your physical self was unaware. For those who become aware during their life on earth it is a wonderful opportunity to take time and think before acting unwisely. It is easier said than done, even with this knowledge, for one can get caught up in the midst of life which seems to be lived at a faster rate nowadays, and before one realises it the day is over and one can only look back at what happened during those waking hours.

You all asked to come to the earth to have this special experience and what an opportunity it is. You may live different lives, live in different parts of the world but, in this age of communication, you can learn very easily about life all over the world, learn the truths of natural law and spiritual life from the Masters who have lived and are living on the earth. They have all taught that one's own truth is to be found within, for the Spirit, God, resides in everyone and all life, so one can experience peace and love within.

When you go within it may not be like reading a book; however, you will open up links to spirit and to other like-minded people on earth which will result in you receiving spiritual knowledge in different ways. Avenues will open and you will have the opportunity to serve God and your fellow man. You will also have the opportunity to find out who you really are, why you are here and what your life was intended to be. As you become more deeply involved you will receive spiritual sustenance as you meditate and spend time with your Father God.

Your life will be fulfilled as you follow the promptings of your heart and, when your earthly days are over, you will look forward to reliving your earthly life for you will have found the secret of life on earth.

Utopia! That is what all people on the earth desire. They may put it in different words, but even those who use violence for their aims have their own form of utopia. When you hear the word 'utopia' it probably means to you something very wonderful, peaceful, loving, beautiful, another word for heaven. It is natural and inborn in you but, depending upon your state of mind, where you were born, the family you grew up with, your past lives, your current projected life plan, things can alter and make the word utopia mean different things to different people. Life on earth is meant to be utopia, for you all seek betterment in your own lives.

It is good that people on earth have aims for their own meaning of utopia. This keeps one looking forward, investigating, finding out what one can do to reach utopia, for it is not only a desire but it can be thoughts for others, hoping that things will improve for mankind. By the mere fact of coming together with love in your hearts you are living your own utopia, for heaven is not a place. Heaven is within you; it is the spirit within and when you manage to align body, mind and spirit in love then you will have found your heaven on earth.

There are many distractions on your earth today as people invent more and more electronic devices. As they look for more sources of power, as life becomes faster, they try to keep up with the current speed of life. In fact, the way to heaven is to slow down, take time to *be*, find out what is behind life, and find the unconditional love that you are, that is your spirit. When people find this, they no longer need to keep up with the Jones's, or stay in the rat race. They will still need jobs, of course, in order to provide for their families, but they will have a different view of life. They will realise that it is more important to think of others, through their own thoughts within, than to be forever chasing their own tails for the elusive heaven that they think is out there.

Once you discover that the basis of life is within, you will probably enjoy life more through the simple things, because that is where you find spirit. You look at the sea and observe its beauty and colours. It may be a raging sea or it may be very calm, but you know that the water making up the sea is one of the main elements of the earth. It is God Himself, as are all elements.

The true purpose of life is to find and realise the love that you are, to experience love in both receiving and giving. To receive you give, and when you give love without condition you have realised the purpose of your time on earth. You will have felt heaven within because you cannot give without receiving, receiving love, receiving peace and receiving contentment.

Why in your world does one country have more than sufficient resources and food and another very little? We know you all dream of equality in the sense of having sufficient money and resources to feed the populations of these countries. However, there is a lot more to it as you are no doubt aware.

Apart from the disparate levels of wealth in the various countries, how would people have different lives looked at from so many points of view? How would they spend a life of luxury in a desert? How would they spend a life without, or with very little, food in a rich country? People on our side of life even request to incarnate in poor countries to experience life there.

There are pockets within the rich capitals of the world where people are starving. Have they requested it? Is it their karma, or is it chance? There is no 'chance' in your world. There is a plan and it takes everybody to make up your world, so don't be too sorry when people are experiencing a lack of food. There are ways that you can help, and you do help, but if everything was turned on its head and those who were supposed to experience difficult times in terms of finance and food were suddenly supplied with riches how would they gain the experience that they were meant to in this lifetime? Conversely, if someone supposed to have a life of luxury with limitless funds lost everything, how would they experience the life they were supposed to?

We can go on and on because sometimes people do lose everything and, yet, that is supposed to happen in their lives. Really, we come back to the fantastic world in which you live. It has everything: it has a multitude of lives and, as everyone chose for themselves the type of life they wanted, there is really no need to feel sorry for them. Nevertheless, when you send out your love you are trying to help those who seem less fortunate than yourselves.

While we are not suggesting you ignore what is going on in the world we just reaffirm that the things that happen are meant to happen. Remember, it is all in the plan.

Truth to everyone is different according to their understanding, but there is one undiluted Truth and that is God Himself. What may have been true to you ten years ago is now different as you have moved on, become nearer to the God within, nearer to your real self and, in so doing, your understanding has moved on apace. There is so much to learn, and one never stops.

On our side of life, also, there are such differences in understanding on the various levels. As we near the higher levels we, too, are privileged to hear further truths, which resonate within us progressively as we become closer to the Great Spirit.

Truth is a huge subject, in the sense of what truth is to you individually, but it need only be simple. If you adhere to the truth you will make headway on the earth plane, for the truth is within you and is as it should be at that particular moment. As you follow the truth within you will make strides yourself and open up to find even greater wisdom.

It is said that one can find everything within, but how is that? Many people cannot; they hear the words, they go inside and hear nothing. It is a matter of listening and persevering; it is a matter of leaving the outside world behind you and being in that chosen space. You may not hear words directly, but you will have impressions at least and they will leave something within your heart centre.

When the time is right those impressions will turn into thoughts and words. As you go deeper in meditation, when you have lost yourself completely, you will reach a stage where there is an opening within and you will see a vast vista of colours and have blissful feelings. Then, if you continue further, the picture will become clearer and you are open to receive. Again, you may not receive the actual words, but keep at it. You will be taking in knowledge whether you realise it or not, so that another day, a month or two down the line, something will click within you and become, as you call it, a new truth.

So, be happy with your truth as it is at the moment but seek always for higher teachings.

We wish to say a few words about the layers of light, layers in the spirit world. Layers, or levels as they are sometimes called, conjure up various imaginings in different minds. The ones to which we refer are transparent but, nevertheless, when in those layers you can feel them tangibly. There are many, many, more layers than you could ever dream of, for the spirit world is so expansive and, compared to the physical, very large indeed. Being spirit there is no size in reality but, for your minds, you need to equate this with something you are used to. Therefore, to use the word layers seems appropriate.

We are speaking to you from, shall we say, a middle to higher layer. This is where there is such beauty, where thoughts are pure but we still have humour; we can have pure humour. We understand your humour having lived on the earth at some stage, or many stages in most cases. We feel the purity of air, that freshness you get on earth at dawn. It is not air, for we do not need air, but we do experience all the best of earth plus almost the best of spirit. We look to raise ourselves towards the ever-brighter light as do all who return to spirit once they become aware and have recovered from their sojourns on earth.

For those who have had, shall we say, difficult lives on earth they know not where they are when they come to spirit. They think their lives have ended and many of them sleep, in terms of your earth time, for a long while. As they gradually emerge from their confused state we, on our side of life, are ready. We are waiting for them to emerge; we take them by the hand and show them they have nothing to fear. We introduce them to their surroundings which are sometimes very poor indeed, but we give them love, we give them shelter, we bring them gradually into our way of life.

From those early beginnings they have within the need to progress, for we tell them and show them how bright it is as they climb up the various layers. They are encouraged, for they see not only their friends but lightworkers, as we shall call them, who will stay with them as a form of service, take them through their early days and show, in graphic detail, their previous life. The lightworkers give comfort to the soul who has passed, as dawning arises within them, for they may feel concern about many things from their life. Criticism is not necessary, as there is no better learning than through oneself. They are given all the love they need and, as they begin to understand more, other helpers and lightworkers are sent, and so this continues.

We now give an example of someone who has spent their life in service to others. Upon passing, their transition will be easy. It will be as though they were waking up to beautiful sunlight, green fields, an array of flowers; in fact, just like being in the next room or the next house, but they will know where they are for they will be given the understanding within. They will be greeted by their friends, relations and people who have known them in previous lives. There will be such a celebration for the life just led and, in earth terms, there will be the equivalent of a large banquet. Everyone attending will rejoice to receive their relation and great friend back in the land of light.

In reality there is, of course, no time in spirit, although it will appear to be so. Most souls, such as the one just mentioned, will not need any adjustment, but will enjoy getting used to their new living arrangements. Nevertheless, they will still have within that desire to rise to the next layer. Many, many opportunities are given to everyone here to serve the Great Spirit. They may be given difficult tasks, just as you are on earth, but they are carried out willingly, with love and without concern.

We wish to talk about progression, progression of the human species – called evolution by your scientists – and progression of the soul, the soul of life. The soul takes you between different incarnations and beyond, which you may have heard about, for there is far more to your lives than the earth and the immediate spirit world. Looking at your physical universe, and how limitless it is, don't you think there must be more? Of course, you may also have heard of other universes, spiritual universes, and these, too, are limitless.

Reincarnation is much spoken of nowadays, quite often in jest, but many really wonder if they will come back as a dog or an ant or something. Rest assured, this does not happen and you progress from one kingdom to another. For instance, you may once have been a rock in the mineral world and subsequently evolved through the vegetable, animal and human kingdoms.

People talk about leaving the earth and entering the astral realms. You probably think the astral realms are the closest spiritual counterpart to the earth and this is right. Some people, when they pass over, spend a long, long time in the astral realms. Others, who have led important, interesting and uplifting lives can go straight to the higher realms: not the higher, higher realms, but the next link above the astral levels.

Once you have settled into your new spiritual home you will have the opportunity to go beyond the immediate levels, into other physical and spiritual realms because they are linked. You may spend your next life on another planet, not in a physical sense but, rather, in a spiritual sense, for how can you see physical life on a planet like Mars; but there is spiritual life on all the planets.

Keep an open mind; realise there is so much out there, or rather, in there, for you will attain everything through the inner world, the inner world of the soul, of the spirit, for they are at One. The soul is used, like the mind, to record not only your actions but your thoughts and your feelings.

Your lives are themselves limitless; think of infinity and they are even beyond that. The human mind cannot take in the physical universe let alone the thought of spiritual universes. However, there is no need to dwell on this, just be aware that there is so much ahead of you, ahead of your life in whichever dimension you will next be.

So, look forward with confidence, with joy, with love, to each moment you have left on earth and also your future lives.

In human terms, it is said that consciousness passes to the next world as life after death. So, what is human consciousness? It is the whole being; body, soul and spirit. Obviously, the physical body is left behind at death, but you are made up of several bodies, or sheaths. As you progress in the spiritual dimension you move into these different bodies which become finer and vibrate at a higher rate. Each of these bodies enables you to move within the levels of spirit.

Although you can visit the lower realms to help, teach, comfort and generally assist those coming to terms with their new lives, you cannot advance to the higher realms until your soul is ready. As you move up to each new level the light is so bright you cannot stay there unless you are ready and have earned your progression. Great teachers, Masters of light, come down to see you and, in turn, teach and encourage you with new knowledge and experiences. Their bodies appear so bright you can only look at them when you are ready. Nevertheless, you are aware of them when they visit your level.

Just as you leave your physical body when moving to spirit, so you cast off each of the ethereal bodies as you progress on this side of life. When in the physical body you are consciousness, but you are not aware of this until you look beyond the body and raise your understanding and awareness of other dimensions; universes, if you like.

It is possible, in the physical dimension, to expand your being beyond the physical but you will always be tied to the body with what is sometimes called the 'silver cord' until you are ready to move back to the spirit world. This will not occur until you have completed your allotted time and experienced all you came to earth for. You all face different lives and times on earth, for each of you has a unique blueprint which covers the parents you chose, location, certain events and people you meet. It includes your education, type of work and religious and spiritual aspirations. It encompasses the whole spectrum of your life on earth and, although you have free will, you will broadly stay within the parameters of your own blueprint.

Your blueprint was determined by a free will discussion before you came to this life on earth. Nevertheless, within the blueprint there is scope for you to expand your service opportunities and other avenues of interest that appeal to you. You most certainly are not like robots. You have intelligence, you have a mind and brain, enabling you to think, plan and judge or go beyond the senses as you expand into the realms beyond the physical. Your brains have untapped areas which come into play with this expansion of your being into other realms.

As you make use of your new-found knowledge, wisdom and closeness to the Great Spirit this has a positive bearing on the rest of your brain. It brings joy, youthfulness and happiness into your life which reflects in your eyes, on your face, in your demeanour, overall personality and relationship with others. The opportunities are limitless within your consciousness, as you live out your life and receive from the physical and spiritual realms. You are preparing your new home in spirit by the manner, openness, and, of course, the love you share with all you meet and those beyond your immediate surroundings.

The more you expand your whole life through love and service the more you will realise that consciousness is limitless. It will take you forward in wholeness and Oneness beyond your thoughts, aspirations and wildest dreams.

People often question why a few individuals commit what appear to be dreadful acts of violence in the name of religion. The great majority of people in the world abhor this and all acts of terrorism. Why do they do it? Coupled with that question people ask why God allows these things to happen. As the answers to both are linked, we will take the second part first and then return to the first question.

God, the Great Spirit as He is often called, is not a man sitting in judgement organising everything that goes on between people. He is the Creator and Maintainer of all life; He is Love itself and has set in motion the universe, including the earth, to work with amazing precision.

We will consider the words 'free will', for we are told that everyone has free will. If we take this in its simple meaning, everyone can do anything, good or bad. You are each faced with many decisions every day, some little ones, some big ones and, occasionally, some very difficult ones. You can be affected by everyday living, what you read and what you see on television.

You may be aware that the term free will is more complex than it appears; however, if you intend to do something you could do it. Why does God allow this? The answer is because all of you are God. It is difficult to accept that the God essence is within you until you have complete understanding. When you become totally aware you will *know* that you, too, are God. To get to the stage of realising that one is God takes many, many lives and we do not expect you to act as though you are God, for you each have your own pathways.

If you can accept for a moment that you are God, from your situation and love for humankind you would not allow such atrocities to take place. The majority of people do not realise they are God and, therefore, need to learn many lessons in life. The most important of these is that there is no death, only what appears like a movement from one room to another, the transition from the physical state to the spiritual. From this perspective the act of someone losing their earthly life can be viewed in a more philosophical way and offers assurance to one who is unaware that life continues.

God has set and continues to set everything in motion with His love. He allows free will and, therefore, He would not prevent things happening for it would upset the balance of His creation. That does not mean that you and He do not have compassion, for He has given it to you in your make-up. Each person develops their own characteristics and it is by showing compassion and love that one grows. Remember, before you came to the earth you had a blueprint for your life which you agreed, so in that sense you had free will then, although part of what happens on earth may not appear to be free will. There are many factors involved in free will, but when at One with God you appear to have given up free will because all your actions and thoughts are those of the Creator.

We understand completely your compassion over atrocities but, remember, there is much more to it than appears. Everyone learns from these actions and it is how one deals with life as a result of them that really counts. Have you noticed that people are brought together and so much help and love is evident after these events?

Let us remember who brings us all together, for we sometimes forget the Great Spirit is always here without fail. You on the earth plane and we in spirit sometimes forget who is responsible for all life, created the universe and all life forms on it. Mankind has been part of the Great Spirit since time immemorial, not necessarily in the form you now recognise but held within and containing the Great Spirit, for where you have one drop of Divinity you have Totality.

Totality is not felt by the majority of people, although occasionally it can be experienced when making a special connection within. It can occur when enjoying music and be projected from the eyes if you are viewing art, nature or the landscape, but the reaction is always within.

So, where does the Great Spirit feature in one's everyday life? Most people are not aware, and even if they pray to their God they often think of Him as being outside of themselves. Those who are aware that God is within all life have the opportunity to use that knowledge as they go through life. It is all too easy to get caught up in the pressures of the day and to forget. Yet, the odd thing is that when concentrating or being immersed in some project they are at One with the Creator.

From a conscious point of view how can one remember that the Lord is with one at all times? In your busy lives you are not expected to meditate for long periods, but the more you are able to spend time sitting still, contemplating, thinking, the more you will find that you have an automatic thought, notion, feeling, awareness, that your God is with you at all times. Can you imagine having that conscious awareness always; would it not be amazing?

The more you can spend time within the more this conscious awareness will become part of your day and the more this happens the easier it will be for you to follow your pathway. Even so, when you are aware that your God is with you all the time, you still have free will but you will not feel the need to think of it. By walking hand in hand with the Lord, everything that you would have wanted from free will automatically takes place.

Are you ready? Are you ready to let go and let God direct your life, or are you only thinking about it and putting it off for another day?

Are you ready? Are you ready to let God direct your life, to let God live through you?

He is you. He is within you and if you let go your life can become a revelation. It will not be what you expect, for the ways of God may seem strange to those on earth, but Godliness is the way forward. When you are ready, when you *are* ready, relax and let God into your innermost secrets. Let Him into your happy moments, your sad moments, your difficult moments.

He is always ready. He is you, He is in you and He is living through you. When you open yourself to God's true Spirit then your life will take on unimagined abundance, for the greatest intelligence in the universe is able and willing to work through you and with you. It only takes a moment to let go, let go of your problems, let go of everything that worries you.

Let go and let God; let God be you. You don't have to think of Him all the time; you just need to be aware and have that open feeling, allowing Him…

Who is doing the allowing, anyway? Who is there?

God is in all life, whether you realise it or not, so to open yourself and *be* God's life will mean a feeling of change coming over your body. You will feel upliftment; you will feel warmth, especially around your heart area, and that warmth will go through your body and your mind. You will be directed by God and He will open doors you didn't think possible. You will walk through those doors and see and feel wonder upon wonder.

So, are you ready? A simple answer in the affirmative will change your life forever.

Chapter Four

Ready to Serve

Miracles: What do you think is a miracle? Is it a newborn babe? Is it a bud of a flower opening up, or is it something unusual, something that goes beyond scientific laws? We say to you that it is all these things and, in any case, who creates scientific laws, but man?

Really, we are saying that miracles are things or actions that happen and are caused by forces other than the human body. They are actions of God, and you are right to describe a newborn babe as a miracle. When you think of it, it really is amazing, not just with a baby child but with all new life, for it brings love and compassion to mind. When a new plant flowers for the first time, man thinks he has done it by just putting it in the ground after buying it but, of course, it is your Creator who prepares the plant and grows it by providing water and food so that the plant knows when to provide the flowers. Don't you think it is incredible? Also, you don't usually have just one flower on a plant; you have so many that sometimes you cannot even count them. So, yes, that too is a miracle.

Where do you think the healing you have been privileged to take part in, and be channels for, comes from? It is other than the physical, isn't it? You feel energies within yourself when you are giving healing in various ways; the recipient invariably feels something and generally is uplifted, peaceful, and knows that. Yes, a miracle has taken place.

However, people don't always get better, for if it is the Lord's will that it is someone's time to go to spirit then, despite whatever help he or she is given, that will be the end result. Nevertheless, many people who have received spiritual healing in their latter days remember it, especially as they are passing to the next world. You could say it is the most supreme healing when one is able to assist in this way. The energy given eases the process for the soul that is passing, and for us as we receive the new soul to our side of life. So, yes, healing is also a miracle.

How would you describe the inspired words given in these meetings, whether written, spoken, received by thought within, or channelling as we are calling it? Yes, it is a miracle, for if you sat down without any preparation or without our help and, above all, without the will of the Father, then you would not be able to channel. So, yes, that too is a miracle.

What about eating and digesting, breathing and the action of the heart pumping blood throughout the body? All these things only take place because of the will of God. We could go on and on in describing miracles, but one of the most satisfying ones for us is when a human being first knows – not believes but knows – that there is more to life than the body. When that human being realises there is a God, the Great Spirit or the mass of energy controlling everything in the universe, when someone first has that knowing then their body is uplifted, as are we when we are able to witness this.

You have all experienced it, and we are not referring to normal religious upbringing. As good as this may be, an individual should find out for him or herself what it means to know that there is a God and to begin the journey of being at One with all life. We feel that this is, and can only be, the principal miracle of all.

As dawn breaks, the sun appears in the east very slowly until the whole orb is visible; light once again descends upon the earth. Mankind awakes to another day, but how many people awaken the light within them? To those who are already awake to the spirit within, to the Great Spirit within all life, it is normal when waking to pray and praise the Lord and give thanks for a new day.

Unfortunately, the majority of people are only concerned with one thing when they rise and that is to prepare themselves for the new day and what they need to do. There is usually a mad scramble on work days and, in this fast-moving commercial world with communications at one's fingertips, there seems little time in which to sit back and reflect on life. On rest days many people are recovering from the rigours of the working week and try to enjoy themselves by living in the fast lane, partying and filling their time with the pleasures available in today's world.

Many do not have time to reflect on their lives during their leisure time. Their working week and times off are usually filled to the brim with activities so they have no time to wonder where their lives are heading and the reason for their lives. They are certainly experiencing life on earth, and often, wonder where their youth and early adulthood disappeared. Even into middle age their lives often continue at a pace. So, unless people are pulled up suddenly in life due to an accident, the death of someone close, or a complete change in lifestyle, it is not until later that the majority of people begin to question what lies ahead of them in this and the next life.

Some belong to the major religions of the world and are active participants in prayer and praise of the Lord; others find the Great Spirit within, for there are many ways, many pathways that lead people back to their Creator. On the other hand, there are so-called religious people who only give lip service to their chosen religion and don't have the all-important awakening feeling within. However, there are those who spend hours in volunteer work, helping and serving mankind. They usually find that their life takes on a real purpose and they receive much more out of life than they appear to give. Sometimes, unwittingly, they find this relationship with their fellow man has led to a deep feeling within them, extending towards all people.

So, through service in life, and following various enforced changes, people begin to question the reason for living and, also, what is beyond the physical. It is at times like these when help is there for them: the spoken word, the written word, chance meetings, books, television and radio, and social media. When people are ready for answers the Great Spirit provides these through many different sources.

As life on earth becomes ever-faster, the day is coming when so many will be abruptly forced to question themselves as changes take place in their lives. With the current and future pace of living something has to give. We, in spirit, are helping bands of people, who have offered themselves in service to the Great Spirit, to prepare themselves for a big influx of people who find themselves suddenly lost in life and require answers, compassion and healing as they experience the glorious opening up of their real selves. They, too, will begin to see their Creator in all life.

People are on earth to learn. They are on earth to live their lives according to the progress they expected when they left the spirit world to be born on the stage of earth.

Yes, it is a stage, and if only people realised it they would not get so angry and upset for they would know that people are playing their parts. Think back to when you enjoyed a good play: you almost became the characters the actors played but, nevertheless, you realised all along that they were only playing a part. The players were *not* the characters they were portraying; they were still their normal selves.

How can one describe a normal self? You can't because there is no such thing as a normal person; all are unique. Isn't that wonderful? What a boring place it would be if everyone was normal, if everybody was the same. So, keep your hearts lifted; rejoice and know that you are playing your part as best you can and, when you return to our side of life, you will enjoy looking back and knowing how well you played your role. Some people play them too well, but others seem to fail, for they are somehow too timid and they suffer because they do not get out of life all that they came for.

However, some of you can see what you have come for. You appreciate the beauty of flowers, you appreciate all of nature, you appreciate the beauty of people, you appreciate the beauty of animals and you appreciate the beauty of spirit within. How can one teach others to feel the same, to experience beauty within, notwithstanding they have their own lives to live, their pathways? If only they could know and see what some of you see it would help them on their way.

Many young souls inhabit your planet at this time but, for most, it is too early for them to have experienced spiritual understanding. Nevertheless, they have spirit within: they are all spirit, but do not realise. They have the same love within them as everyone does, but many don't show it. A lot of this is to do with upbringing, and you know yourselves how you have been conditioned by your early lives. That is part of the pattern of life and that is what is meant to happen, but once one goes past those early years and takes on the responsibilities of life for oneself then a huge difference can be made.

People just seem to go aimlessly through life, whatever age they are, until something happens to shake them to the core. That is when they need people to help them, to advise them, to take them by the hand and show them things they did not know existed.

We are delighted that you are open and ready to help. You may think that you have done enough in this life, but there is never a limit. That is the problem: people have their own limits, but once they remove them life becomes unbelievable. Their lives can develop from within; can take them to avenues new and, normally, unknown on earth, and we can take them to the secrets of the unseen universes.

You have touched on this, and you will see more in time for you are ready; you are always open and seek to learn, we know. Just let go a little more when you are on your own. When you have a few moments of peace go into the silence; come to us and we will take you beyond the barriers you have made for yourselves. We look forward with relish to taking you to places new.

Many people in your world today feel confused about life and the purpose of it. They see what is going on all around them; they see the troubles in the world and they experience problems themselves. Some have tried religion and, indeed, certain ones find solace, a purpose and a reason for their life in their chosen religion. Others, including those who have never been interested in religion, are looking for something they do not know exists.

They are looking for answers and the meaning of life. They do not understand why people should spend a certain number of years on earth and then, in their minds, disappear forever when they die. They cannot believe in a God who would let disasters happen, and yet, when the time is right, they will sense and make enquiries into the fact that there must be a force greater than man behind life on earth and the universe.

Yes, many people are crying out to a God, who they probably don't believe in, to help them understand not only what their life is about, but also the purpose of it. Changes on the earth or, more specifically, changes in the conditions of life on earth, are happening at a faster rate than at any time in its history. You are seeing migration on a large scale and fanatics who believe they have the answer to life on earth through violence. Your communications are so advanced that you know what is happening on the other side of the world almost before it takes place.

There is, therefore, a great need today for people who have an understanding and a connection with their God within, to offer themselves in service to mankind by opening their souls to All That Is. They live their lives according to the understanding, beliefs and knowledge they have gained from within. Time will be found for those people to be used in different ways, according to their different personalities. They will be used in the quiet of their homes as they send out love and healing to the world. They will be used in their normal lives by being examples to those around of the way they live their lives. They will show by the light in their faces and a glint in their eyes that they have found the answer to life on earth.

They will be in touch with one another, not necessarily physically or by earthly communications, but through the ways of the Great Spirit for He created contact between all life. For millions of years this connection has been in existence and, from time to time with different civilisations, man has used this communication to further the evolvement of man on earth. Now, the time for this to happen has arrived again. You do not need to try to make contact for the communication is already there. All that is necessary is to become more at One, firstly through meditation and, secondly, by giving your whole self in love to the Great Spirit.

In this way you open your own connection, and the more you can do this the more your lives will become integrated between all mankind. You do not have to do anything physically; it will just happen and you will be aware within of the communication and communion. From there you will know that, whatever happens within, the unseen spiritual connection will manifest itself outwardly in your lives. You will find that you will be placed in certain situations where you are able to help many souls, who will then be ready to learn more of the spiritual side of life and the unseen workings of God.

Continue to open up within and you will see and experience the wonderful world of spirit. As you begin to meet more and more people, in various situations, you will have all the necessary words at your disposal to fulfil the real purpose of your incarnation.

The leaders of your world are once again saying how powerful they are, and what will happen… If!

They are threatening, instead of sending love. This is a continual problem on your earth. The power that goes to people's heads when they feel in charge of a great mass of land – which isn't really theirs anyway – seems to make them behave in a way that causes problems for other leaders. They, in turn, feel the need to respond and so the earth seems to go from one crisis to another.

Unfortunately, journalism makes hay of this and your papers have been, and are, full of the dangers involved: the possibility of world war again. In fact, if anything, the world of journalism seems to thrive on this sort of problem, on the angry confrontations between nations. Where is the love, the forgiveness? That is down to groups who wish and pray for peace, but it is no good praying for peace when in your mind you are taking sides, when you are filling your brain with all the latest news of what could happen.

The way to deal with these situations is to be aware of the problems but not go into great detail, not listen to all the news channels. Instead, feel the love and peace within and send out that love and peace. Beyond that, be peaceful yourself, show by your acts of kindness, by your love, that this is the way forward and, as you do this, it will spread. To dwell on all the negative happenings in your world is not the solution. The answer is to have peace and love in your mind and in your heart, so that when you think, speak, and act, your words will be of peace, of kindness, of help, of comfort and, yes, of love.

Be happy, and you will see your world as something beautiful; you will see your world as it was meant to be seen. Such beauty, such delicate flowers, beautiful fresh air, the wonderful colours of the oceans, the sky, the forests, the mists, and the rays of the sun. That is the world to which you belong, so make it your world. When you live with peace and love in your heart you are doing more than all the politicians who come together to try and obtain peace; although, of course, action is needed.

We say again, if more and more people can live and act in this way the world will change very quickly. For your sake, make your own world. See it as love, as beauty, and your life will be the same.

As you sit with your thoughts – or without your thoughts if you are waiting to be inspired – you feel relaxed, for you are all receptors and transformers because you have lived your lives in such a way that you have peace in your hearts. You do not continually think, why did I do that? Why did I do this? You may sometimes have those feelings but, overall, you know that your thoughts have been for others. You have looked after yourselves as you needed to but your feelings, when you hear of distress in others, go straight to them. So, you can sit and relax without feeling guilty, without feeling that you have to do something.

As you are in this position you are receptors; you receive from us and you receive from others. Then you are transformers, for you have lived varied lives and you have experienced many difficulties from which you have learned. Therefore, you have transformed yourselves throughout your lives but, more importantly, you are helping to transform others because, as you give out and they receive, they wonder how you or others can do and say things and live the way you do. This has a snowball effect; the mere fact that you can sit not only in circle, but at any time without fear and without guilt, means that you can absorb so much more. People who have worries on their minds all the time find themselves unable to take in that from which they would otherwise benefit.

Throughout life there is give and take. Some seem to give more than others, but all give and take to a degree. Those who seem to give more also appear to be the happiest, for they are not thinking of themselves. They are thinking of others and you know that when you get together with others and help people there is a wonderful feeling of togetherness. You all have different lives, you all have different experiences. As you go through this life, seek more knowledge and, when it comes to you, be ready and willing to share with all who care to listen.

It is not just speaking: in fact, the greatest teaching is by example where no words take place. People ask themselves, 'Why is he or she always so happy?' 'Why can't they be like us?' There is some envy, but if they ask and dig deeper they will see the reason for themselves. So, be happy that you are able to sit alone, or together, and feel at peace, for that peace is within you, is within everyone. However, only a small percentage are able to show peace on their faces, to show peace in what they say, for the great majority are always looking for sound, looking for excitement, looking to do something, to play something, when they can find all they need within.

We are not suggesting that you don't go out and enjoy yourselves; this is part of what life is for. Life is to experience but, at the end of the day it is to find and give out the love that you are, for you are the Great Spirit and you were made in His image. What does that mean? Most people think that they have to look like God; nobody knows what God looks like so that is very difficult. The nearest we can say is if you are made in His image then you feel, say, think, and do as you believe God would.

Now, we know that God is above all that. He is all life, the whole universe, and He would not think like you or act like you, so we really have a conundrum here. How would God feel? He just *is;* everything *is* and it is people who make things complicated. That is why we say you can be at peace with your thoughts, at peace with your actions, at peace with your friends and at peace with your enemies. Most of you don't think of enemies so we will describe enemies to you as negative thoughts. You have shown that you send out your love not only to victims but also to perpetrators and that is a very difficult thing to do, especially if one is personally involved in some cruel action.

We will sum up by saying continue to relax within your spirit. Whenever you are unsure then go within and feel as you do now and you will receive any help that you need. Continue being a catalyst for peace, friendship and love by the way you live.

We are dwelling for a few moments with you in the quiet, for in that quiet you can find the Great Spirit. You can find the engine room of your life, of your body; you can find all you need. It is not a question of asking and getting an immediate answer; that would be too easy. It is a matter of your attitude and your understanding, for the Great Spirit knows what you need and gives you what you need. When you think you *need* something you will not necessarily receive, for it is not the need your soul desires. However, when it is part of your life plan then it will come to you. You will also receive what is needed for any given situation, for what you are doing, for what you will need to do and for the extra you will need when giving service.

Much has been said about healing and you know you activate healing the moment you think of someone. Whether you ask for help, or not, the mere thinking of that person or situation brings the love and energy that makes up the healing; however, true healing takes place when the physical is absent. In other words, when one is in touch with the God within, the spirit within you as a healer will contact the soul and spirit of the one to whom you are giving healing.

Now, the spirit in all is perfect, but it is surrounded by so much negativity in some people that they never allow it the chance to illuminate them. It is not just about healing the physical: it is so important to heal the invisible in the person, to heal not only the thoughts but the whole being.

Someone once said that complete healing does not take place unless the receiver is aware of its source, and is given the deeper understanding of the Great Spirit. So, when you are giving healing do take every chance to speak the words that are given to you. You only have to open yourselves to us, both for the healing and the words, and you will know what to say.

It is our pleasure to be with you this evening. We bring our love and it is mingling with yours as you think of those in need across the world, for there are so many in your world today who need assistance: spiritual assistance as well as medical assistance. It is easy to be distracted in your world and think it is not a good place to be; you, however, realise more. You understand that you make your own world, for you recognise that all is One, that the part of you that connects to all life is the spirit, the life, the joy of life, and you consequently aim to see the good in life.

Far too many see negativity, which affects their own lives to a large degree. If only they would view life as a whole, look at the good things in life, they too would have a world surrounded by love and joy, for beauty is all around. It is there to be seen by those with eyes to see. Many experience some of the beauty in life, but in going beyond the physical you can also see the spiritual part, thereby deriving much more pleasure when looking at a country scene, looking at the sea, and viewing the stars at night.

You take pleasure in all you see, for you realise that God is within everything He has created and continues to create. Be proud that you can see beauty all around, you can see truth in life and you can see love, not hatred. With your eyes you can see goodness in all things. Yes, you can be affected by tragedies but, overall, you see more of the full picture. You see that you are here to experience love and you are here to serve. You are here, above all, to find your real self within.

We bring beauty in a breath to you, we bring beauty in a raindrop to you. We bring beauty in the sun's rays to you and we bring beauty in the silence.

Today, you have brought your whole selves and left behind the unimportant stuff, the stuff that will be there for another day. So, being all together in spirit gives us a pure circle of love, the love of the Father which is in each of you and us, the love that dominates all in its path and turns everything into pure white: a love that can only be dreamt of by most people, a love which goes before one like a lamp lighting the way and clearing obstacles.

The love of the Father, in its purest form, is not felt by most people because of its high intensity, but when you are leading lives of love, when you are thinking of others, when you are helping others, when you are helping the planet, when your desire is service to mankind then you will have that love with you at all times. You will touch on it and feel it and sense it so much that when another is in a similar state you will feel at one with them.

The love of the Father is really indescribable; it is so powerful. When you open to the Great Spirit you are allowing and inviting that love to come into your very soul. Your spirit, of course, is pure love, so when the two join it is like an explosion of light within and this is how we feel the conditions when we all meet like this. We are very grateful and we know you are, too, and as we all go forward with God's love there are no limits to what can be achieved.

We are love; we are God's love, for we are God Himself, but we tend to forget, even us in spirit. Imagine always being aware of the love within you and around you, then your lives would be ecstatic all the time. There is no reason why this cannot be; it is just that the mind comes in and brings one back to so-called reality. The reality is, of course, God's love, God's light; the Reality that is within all life.

We wish to expound on the subject of service. Most people serve in one way or another, but it is how they serve, their attitude, that matters. Is it carried out with love, or out of habit feeling it is something that has to be done? There is a huge difference and that difference is felt by the recipient.

It is such a pleasure to be helped by someone with love in their eyes, love from their heart, that shows in their mannerisms. You all know that when someone is angry you don't need to hear the words; you can tell from their mannerisms. So, it is with service: service with a smile they say, provided the smile is genuine.

Service does not necessarily mean touching people and taking them by the hand. This is, of course, a great help but service can simply be done by sitting still and sending out loving thoughts. When you come together to serve, in one form or another, there is a special feeling between you. For example, you are sitting together now and you have that special feeling.

You may not think you are serving at this moment but you are serving everything all around you, without realising it, when you sit together in love.

When you are serving in this way there is a special relationship between you. It is the same when people join together to tidy a place, do some gardening, or whatever the need. There is companionship and, at the basis of all this is love, that *wanting to give* inherent in every human being. Sometimes it appears hidden, but it is within them, for being part of the Great Spirit you are programmed to give, give, and go on giving and not count the cost.

When you engage in service you feel so uplifted; the whole of your body taking on a special feeling. The oxygen that comes into you has something extra about it; the blood that runs through your veins has an extra vitality. Your whole body receives as you are giving but, above all and more importantly, your personality, your mind, is receiving. This process is ongoing and not only aids progress in this lifetime but automatically prepares one for the next life.

You may say, 'I don't want a next life', but what life are you talking about? Your immediate next life will be with us and I'm sure you want that. No, you're talking about your next earthly life. How do you know if you'll have one? You may have served all the lives you need to; on the other hand, if you are a giver you probably never will give up taking lives on earth.

With each new incarnation you forget all your previous lives on earth. Nevertheless, when you have lived so many lives in service you know inside that contentment, you know inside that eternal peace. In any new life, when you are giving you cannot fail to know the joy that the Great Spirit has given to all who want it. We say all who want it because many shy away from happiness. They shy away from the reality of life, they shy away from expressing themselves openly, they shy away from giving love openly.

The more lives you spend in service to your fellow man the happier you will be in each future life. You will also spend much time with us because you will deserve to be in the garden of Eden. You will have such a wonderful future ahead of you, firstly where you are and, later on, with us.

So, enjoy these moments, these moments now, and all moments. Treasure them for they will be lost to time but they will leave a beautiful musical note, a wonderful chord, on your soul.

Chapter Five

Creation and Science

We join you in love, the love that comes from the Father, the love that will always be: for the Father will never go away. Can one imagine the state of forever? Forever and ever sounds wonderful. It is even longer than infinity but, looking at it another way, God has always been and always will be. However far back you go in records, or within your soul, you will find that God and love have always existed.

People question creation and mankind's beginning, especially when new discoveries are made by scientists. Each year they find that life goes back further, much further than they thought. Mankind has always been, always been in spirit, so how could it be any different, for you are God.

Planet earth is not alone in the physical universe in having life on it. When you go back as far as your memories will take you, and then back, back into the ages and eons before time, God and your spirit were already existing. Your most recent Avatar said that God separated Himself and created man so that He could love Himself. That is correct but, again, was prior to physical creation, before the Big Bang as you call it.

Life was man in the sense of spirit man. How can your minds even consider the possibility of spirit man before creation? The mind cannot, of course, but the spirit mind, spirit man, can understand and that part of you, your spirit and soul, can understand. So, God formed life, other spiritual life, and when creation in the form of humankind took place man was already prepared for life in the physical universe.

Your scientists make it sound as though physical life took a long time to start. In fact, when God decided that a certain life form would start then it just happened. Your scientists will never find the truth of how mankind started on earth for it goes way beyond what they think. It goes back much further than pre-historic man, for when the earth changed and plates moved life started again in a different part of the world. The records of mankind from the early days are now deep in the oceans and within the highest mountains. Rest assured that you, as man, have been around for a very, very, very long time. Even most people in spirit are not aware of how long.

We speak of this because we want to make the point that love, God's love, has always been. When you feel His love within you, you will know that you, too, are God for there is something special when you can touch on the Holy Spirit within. It expands within your heart area and when you continue to have this wonderful connection you will understand that you are timeless.

When one accepts timelessness why worry about what will happen in the next few hours, in the next few days? People will know that, overall, nothing can touch their real self and, therefore, they can take this wonderful connection of the spirit with them in whatever they are doing and in whatever challenges they meet.

Let them be positive and happy in the knowledge that everything is as it should be.

All things are of the Great Spirit who is, of course, limitless and provides the basis for pure love, for deep peace, for silence; yet contains all power, the nucleus of energy.

You speak of various energies; natural ones like wind, man-made ones like electricity and nuclear power, but at the base of all energy is the Great Spirit the source of love, for everything contains love. Nothing would happen in your world, or in the universe, without love. There is natural law which you could say was formed to control all life; we would rather say natural law is part of God and has always been.

It is said that God created all life. He has always been, so life has always been. Here we are not talking about physical life but, rather, refer to the spirit within all life. There is only God and His natural process. The point we are making is that everything just *is*. As there is no time in spirit and, consequently, no time within all life itself, it follows that everything without time just is, was, and will be.

On earth you make so much of time, for you need time to live by, to follow the action of day and night and we understand why. It would be very difficult to live your lives without that sort of time, but in the scheme of things as there was no beginning and there will be no end, how can there be any time? There always has been life and all you see on earth, including the mountains and the seas, can be likened to your bodies in that they, too, were born and will die: but not so the spirit within.

The Great Spirit is unfathomable and your minds cannot comprehend even an infinitesimal part of His greatness.

Have you ever wondered what or who is behind the movement of the earth, the winds and weather changes? Your immediate reaction can be to say that it is nature. You know, of course, that nature was created, including the earth, the heavens and the whole universe. Why then should the weather be still one day without much movement of wind, the clouds barely moving, and the following day bring strong winds, rain and storm clouds? Certain parts of the world experience extreme weather, hurricanes and very strong winds that cause great damage. As the storms run their course they, in turn, affect different parts of the world.

You may wonder why this is so. God created nature and also natural laws to govern life, not only on earth but throughout the universe. He also set in place systems to deal with the effects of man's treatment of the earth and nature's own effects from within the earth such as volcanoes and earthquakes. Nevertheless, because God created natural laws something more must cause the problems that you see on earth. Naturally, the movement of the earth revolving and making subsequent movement in the atmosphere has an effect. However, other difficulties are often related to the behaviour of people on earth.

All thoughts and actions have results. It is not surprising, therefore, that you see changes on your earth today. Only when people themselves start thinking of others, caring for and loving one another and all living creatures, including the earth itself, will natural disasters cease.

The world today is troubled due to the beliefs of certain communities, much of it in the name of religion. Although each religion was founded on love this seems to have been forgotten as the egos of people surface and, as a consequence, the word love is lost to many of them. All people must be aware of the problems today and those who send out peaceful and loving thoughts are helping, so you may wonder why there has been little improvement. However, have you ever considered that, although things may not have changed they have been prevented from getting much worse?

What more can people do? Individually, you can start or continue to look within your own hearts. Make that special place an abode of peace and as you make contact with others so they will feel the peaceful vibrations that you automatically send out. In time, and as more and more people begin to think in this way, attitudes will begin to change.

Have you ever tried to describe the Great Spirit? As a child you were taught that God was a man with a long beard who sat in the heavens and directed all life. Later, you started searching and you realised that there must be more to it: there must be more to a Creator who could produce a universe of unimaginable size which man is still exploring with his space crafts and telescopes and is amazed by its vastness.

What, or who, could create such an awe-inspiring universe? You realise it is not someone like a man. You realise that it is a superintelligence but what sort of superintelligence? People on earth look for images because you live in a physical world and it is very understandable. How can you, therefore, make an image of your God that would satisfy you? We cannot describe the Great Spirit, other than to say He, She, or It, is whatever you want Him, She, or It to be, for He is beyond description. In creating the universe and everything in it He has demonstrated that His power is limitless.

You could ask why He does it, what He is doing now while mankind makes a mess of the earth? Be assured, God created everything necessary to take care of what happens on earth. He created the Lords of Karma so that the results of all actions would be in accord with the natural law of cause and effect. You might say He could sit back and watch what is going on but, of course, He is beyond that. We don't know how He feels because He is beyond feeling. We don't know what He does because He is beyond doing. We don't know what He has in mind for the future, for He is beyond even that.

Some say the Great Spirit has made plans, but this is said in order that your minds can grasp something of His purpose. He is so expansive the human mind cannot get even a miniscule part of the way towards understanding Him. You cannot see the Great Spirit and you cannot understand Him, but you can feel Him within you and within all of life. You experience the sunshine, a beautiful day, raindrops, frost, snowflakes: whatever nature produces it is because of Him. Investigate, if you will, but we suggest the nearest you can come to your God is by loving, loving your fellow man. In this way you are loving God and when you demonstrate your love for God you will receive His love. It is all around you anyway and by your actions, which cause reactions, you cannot fail to receive that love.

Love is within you but you do not always feel it. It is when you concentrate, when you meditate, when you stand back, then you can feel it. You can also feel it helping you, encouraging you, for if you rely one hundred per cent on your God you can achieve anything, and we mean anything! If there is something important for you to do then, remember, with God's grace you can do it.

The earth has an amazing atmosphere which enables you and all life to live; without it there would be no rain and there would be no food to sustain you. Have you looked deeply into clouds, their formation, their different types from the little white fluffs to the heavy dark clouds? When the dark clouds join together the light is reduced, but water falls from them as they become too heavy and the land is refreshed. When the clouds move away you are left with the heat of the sun. There are different seasons and nature adapts to the changes throughout the year.

People take this for granted, but what sort of intelligence foresaw such possibilities in the atmosphere when creating the universe? There are many secrets in the universe. Mankind is only just on the fringe of realising its enormity, how the whole universe is linked and operates so that each planet, each star, is interdependent upon the other. How can anyone understand what intelligence created the universe? Mankind doesn't even understand his own earth so what chance has he to understand the universe?

You are not expected to understand the whole workings of the earth, let alone the universe, but God created man with imagination, with inquisitiveness, and you were given brains and minds in order to find ways of advancing your life and the lives of those around you by serving your fellow man. To enable this to happen man needed to investigate, to invent, and what you see today is the progress that has been made. Whether or not you agree with it is another matter. Not everybody can be a great scientist, but if you are able to use your lives to gain understanding and be eager to help one another then you are living the lives you chose for this incarnation.

There is so much to learn; your explorers now go way down to the bottom of the oceans. They already go way up in the sky but, rather, they need to look at themselves. Everybody needs to look within and find the centre of their being. You have been given all the facilities to live your lives according to your chosen pathways. Many people don't even realise they have a chosen pathway; those who do are in a privileged position. As you come to explore your own minds and souls, explore the beauties within, you will find that your lives will expand and become joyful, and as you help others so you help yourselves.

People say they are ready to help but unsure how to proceed. We would say go within and ask to be shown the way. There are many people who start the day in meditation, asking the Great Spirit for guidance and to be shown what they can do. Before long things will happen, you will hear of friends or others who are in need.

It is always useful to remind oneself of the basics and there is no better way to start the day than in communion with your Father God.

Have you ever thought what makes up the air that you breathe? We don't mean mainly oxygen and nitrogen as the scientists will tell you. No, we mean what *really* makes up the air you breathe. It is, of course, unseen and it is the Great Spirit activating the molecules that make up the air, for without the joining together of these molecules there would be no air in your atmosphere. It would just be dead: it would just be elements in a gaseous state hanging there and it would not be the air you recognise.

The next time you enjoy the beautiful fresh air of the morning remember how it is enabled to be in the form that you recognise, how it is taken into your bodies to activate the movements and complete life of the body. When man thinks he can grow a new life he is far from the truth, for no life exists without the authority and love of the Great Spirit. The tiniest drop of water only exists because of the will of God. Think wider, know that you and all life, including the earth itself and the universe, that multitude of bodies, only exists because of the will of God.

How does this make you feel and how does this knowledge affect your lives? Most people would not give it a thought, but scientists are always looking for reason with their own truth; they seem to miss the fact that the Creator is everywhere and without Him they would not be here. Others are investigating and questioning all aspects of life, not just the physical.

This information adds weight to one's faith, or knowing, that life is more than it seems. Do you think that the Creator would have made life without so many different and interesting aspects? Of course not, for it is in the pleasures and difficulties that the soul grows. If everything was easy then there would be no growth and the more that the soul grows and experiences the more life will become richly fulfilled.

Life, as you know it, is not all it seems. The Great Spirit has made it this way in order that people can eventually go beyond the physical and find the true wisdom behind all things in life. The more one delves into what is behind life the more one finds there is so much more to learn. To be complacent with the knowledge one has does not give the incentive to explore the greater mysteries of life.

To continue searching and learning will result in finding new truths, and your being will be filled with a lasting desire to serve mankind and the Great Spirit.

We bring to you the blessings of pure air and sunshine that we knew in days gone by when we inhabited your planet. We loved the land, the rivers, the moon, the sun, the beautiful sky and, indeed, the clouds. We especially treasured the tall trees that gave us shade.

We bring this purity of air and water to you at this time, for it is needed. Your rivers, your streams, have been polluted over many, many years. Although you are making efforts to cleanse your planet you seem to go two steps forward and three steps backward, for you are not all working together. You have one country making great efforts and you have other, larger, countries that are polluting more each day.

Again, we bring to you the thought of God's pure air and His beautiful, rippling clear waters. With this image you can transform the planet through your minds, through your thoughts, words and deeds. There is much more to life than appears in the physical world, and by your helpful, caring, loving thoughts and actions you can purify your locality and the earth.

Gradually, this movement to cleanse the planet will gather momentum and, in time, mankind also will become pure again, pure in thought and in living. Remember, the earth herself is just as conscious as you of these impurities and lack of love between nations.

Those who live by Divine law are helping the earth, and the earth is aware of it. It is known that where there is life you have feelings which are affected by the thoughts and words of others, whether they are human beings, animals, or even plants. Each feels the effect of thoughts and actions, as does the earth herself, so hold in your minds the beauty of a pure earth for it will return to that state.

Have you ever wondered what the mind is? It certainly isn't the brain, for the brain is a physical organ compared by your scientists to the most advanced computer. The brain, of course, brings in human feelings of love, kindness, and the opposite, negative ones. Scientists are trying to introduce certain feelings as they develop computers more and more, but they will never match the brain in that respect.

So, what is the mind? If we suggest for a moment that the mind is the soul you can say that the soul contains the spirit. People get confused and think of the soul and the spirit as one. In some way it is, because if the spirit is within the human body, and within the mind and the soul, then it is all One.

However, we know people on your earth have inquisitive, enquiring minds and like to put things in separate boxes, so we will continue to use the words brain, mind and soul for your purposes. There are subtle differences between the soul and the mind, but if you consider them as one that will help your understanding.

Of course, within the body, the atoms, the protons and the space within the atoms are all linked to your mind. It is a complex subject, and when you consider that all bodies and all life are connected through the space in the atoms then you can get some idea of the omnipresence of the Great Spirit. There is nothing to stop humans being omnipresent. It is a matter of confidence, knowing, giving up normal desires and going into that special space within.

It is difficult for the human mind to comprehend that part of your soul can be in more than one place at a time. Unless your understanding is advanced you would not be aware that part of you can be elsewhere. However, it is so, and the more you are able to lose your thoughts and be at One with the Great Spirit the more opportunities you will have to experience the wonders in exploration of the mind and spirit.

Masters who lived on earth were themselves omnipresent. To most people and, indeed, to people on a spiritual pathway, the thought that you can be omnipresent may seem far-fetched. However, have you not been in meditation and felt as though you were in another place, had a dream and sometime later been reminded of the experience when not consciously thinking of it. Certainly, when absent healing has been sent out the recipient has been reported to have seen the healer. Again, this demonstrates you can be in more than one place at a time.

We are not suggesting that you spend all your time meditating and trying to be everywhere at the same time! We are letting you know of the possibilities and, in fact, the probabilities that will come in time as more and more people go into their sacred space within.

Our Channel has felt someone close to him this morning who wishes to address us.

'I have been around for a little while today observing the world from your eyes, which takes me back many a long age when I was in your position. The rivers were clean and clear, the forests were green, the air was perfect, always fresh. There were no diesel or petrol fumes, for at that time we were still using horses as our mode of transport; we used to have small ships with sails only. The earth was such a wonderful place.

'All who dwelt in it were mainly healthy and, although they did not have modern technology, they were able to communicate not just by talking to one another but also by an inner communication. We were in contact with our family and friends even though we may have been a few miles away. Our brains and minds were developed so that we could pick up signals. We were also in contact with our ancestors, who were then on the other side of life.

'There was harmony throughout the land, but eventually people were not content living in their own locality and, as always, some wanted more than others. As time went on arguments and wars began and it is a strange thing, you know, that when there are wars men spend their time making more and more armaments because they consider it to be more important than provision for everyday living. Even in your world today there are masses and masses of armaments waiting to be used, enough to blow up your earth many times over. This will not happen because the Great Spirit did not create the earth for it to be blown up. There will still be wars and explosions, but the earth will survive.

'It really is a pleasure to see people living their lives in the way they were meant to. You find harmony among yourselves, among your family, among your friends. You have problems, of course, as do all people, for the earth is a place where their souls can grow. How you deal with problems is important, for the more positive, outgoing and friendly you are and how you behave in these situations, determines your progress.

'Continue to give love and you will find pleasures beyond imagination within. This will, in time, reflect on your outward lives, for if you are peaceful, loving and generous the same will show itself on the outside and, through cause and effect, you will receive similar results.

'It is said that the earth will not return to complete peace and joy for many, many years or lifetimes, but there has to be a start towards this goal and you are making the start that is required. You will know a joyous world, not necessarily outwardly, but within and your lives will be full of happiness and purpose.'

Why is it that colours differ? The reason is that they all come from the great intelligence we call God. In His wisdom He created the whole of the universe and the power that drives it: the power that gives life and light every day. So, it follows that He would create the various colours, all having a purpose and all for a reason.

The perfection of the almighty Spirit knows no bounds. No one can really understand this perfection, but as you become closer to Him you will have some inkling when you receive spiritual thoughts, feelings and see colours. You are given colours when you start meditating, and often people complain that it is just a white light. If only they realised that all colours come from white and radiate into their own distinct ones. As you continue to meditate you will see other colours and when you see mauve or purple you know you are getting near to that perfection. You try to hold onto the experience but, as in all life, if you hold onto things and don't give them out you lose them. Take heart, and when you do receive these blessings be full of thanks and show your gratitude in the only way possible, in your love for God and all His creation.

There are many rays sent to the earth; there are seven main ones and there are also seven within those seven, and a further seven within those and on to infinity. All these rays help to sustain your earth and, indeed, the universe. How else do you think that life could continue in its perfection?

God has created so much that many people have no idea what is behind life on earth. As you become more involved in your quest for closeness with All That Is you will learn of many wonderful rays, rays not only of light but also atomic visions as yet unheard of. Your scientists are not aware of them, but they sustain the rays we have mentioned, the light from the sun and the light inherent in all beings.

There are many views expressed in your world about creation. Your Bible says the world and all life was created in seven days. In whichever way you view the Bible, it was written a long time ago for the people of those times and helped to make sense of how the earth came into being.

Nowadays, people have advanced greatly in terms of understanding the structure and make-up of rock, of animals, of vegetation, and, indeed, the human body, so a more detailed description of creation is really needed. People seem to look at creation in two ways: those who believe there is no God and that everything happened by accident and, on the other hand, those who believe that God created everything. It is a very deep subject, for creation is going on at this moment; it never stops.

People describe the Big Bang with gasses solidifying and forming planets and solar systems within the universe, and from a study of the universe new stars are being created all the time. So, how in your minds could there be nothing and then everything? That's exactly what we are coming to. In God's mind He was *all that ever was*, so He decided to expand and His Spirit is imbued within all physical and spiritual life. Therefore, everyone on earth and in spirit was present at the conception of physical life.

You have seen the wonders of nature, of the seasons, how everything is connected on the earth, how everything works to precision. How could that possibly happen by accident? It could not. We have said before how unbelievably great God is, and the human mind cannot possibly understand Him. It is the same for us, although we have a little more idea, but we do know that there was creation; creation from God's mind which pre-determined every planet, every star, every drop of water on the earth.

Although your minds cannot appreciate how it happened, the fact that there is no physical life without spiritual life means that the Spirit was the Creator, and the magnitude of the physical universe gives you an idea of the greatness of God. There is a thought that there has always been physical life and, in a way, that is correct because within the physical is the spiritual but there was, indeed, a time when God decided to create the universe with all its multiplicities, just like the number of different animals, different species and such a variety in the people of your world.

Creation started so long ago and, whilst it appears that everything is forever growing, especially the universe, this is how it is meant to appear to those who are investigating it from earth. However, it was all created in the beginning and it evolves all the time, but that does not mean that it is getting larger. Again, it may appear that way but the intelligence of God is so vast that the way something appears may not be how it is. The subject of creation is immense, continuing, and will never end.

Mauve colours are pulsating around the room, just like waves. It is the energy you do not normally see but, nevertheless, is all around you, for it is the hidden part of creation. It is what is behind the air, behind the atmosphere, and is the same as the building blocks used for the whole universe. You hear more and more of the wonders of the universe and how long it has been in existence. For instance, the light you now see from a star may have taken many millions or even billions of years to travel through space and reach earth; what you see is no longer happening where it took place. That is the magnitude of the Great Spirit.

At this time, you have no way of travelling by spaceship outside of your own galaxy. Yet, the spirit part within you can instantly travel anywhere, not just within your world, but within the universe and within other universes which can be compared to the spirit world. To you the spirit world is the one you normally associate with the earth, but there are multiple equivalents of earth and there are multiple universes.

Your brains cannot even start to comprehend the power, the enormity of the physical side let alone the unseen side, the spiritual, which you cannot explain in terms of physical space and distance. Be assured that there is so much life, full of power and love, surrounding not just your earth but surrounding the whole universe. The human mind cannot locate the end of the universe; it doesn't know if it is square, round, oval, oblong, or what. It just has an idea of a vast physical area.

Imagine the intelligence that created the universe you are familiar with. Stretch your mind to think of other universes and your mind will truly be scrambled trying to work it out. You are part of that intelligence you call God; that intelligence is you, at the very heart of you.

How many times during the day do you feel the presence of God? Try to remember, whatever situation you are in, to think of the spirit within and you will feel it spreading through your veins, through the whole of your body. The more you do this the more you will find it will be happening automatically, but it does take practice. The spirit part of you is there, always; you hide it when you get so caught up in the events of the day that you are no longer aware of your real being. So, take moments throughout the day, it doesn't need to be a long time, just a few seconds, to feel the presence of God. Gradually you will find that time lengthening so that you become consciously aware of the Spirit within.

Although you are aware at the back of your mind that God is within you, you don't normally experience Him other than in meditation, or unless you happen to be in the presence of a strong spiritual person or in a meeting where like minds come together. Then you have the all-encompassing feeling of the love which is God. Imagine what your lives would be like if you felt that all the time. You know it is possible if you have experienced it, have felt the bliss of how life should be. When you have once felt the essence of all life you wish it to continue.

The more you can do this the more you will be helped in whatever tasks you are undertaking. You will discover the wonder and beauty of the plant and animal kingdoms, and the landscape. You will find it more beautiful and more magnified because, really, you are an integral part of everything and everyone you see. Open your gaze, open your heart, open your being to everything around you and you will begin to feel the Oneness of all life.

The day has dawned, the birds are awake, there is a stillness, a freshness, a beauty, a special time before the demands of the day begin. It is at this time that, without noise and the general cluttering of the mind, one can feel the presence of God.

Today we would speak of the essence of life, the nature of life, the closeness created by the Great Spirit such a long, long, time ago. The essence of life is not seen but is, nevertheless, in all life. It keeps the body operating from the moment the egg is fertilised to the end of earthly life when the life force, consciousness, goes to the world of spirit.

This essence is the missing link that scientists cannot find. They split the atom and continue to search for the microcosm of all life. However, the essence, the life force, is not physical and they will only understand it when they go within and become One with all life, so it is up to spiritually-minded people to bring forth this knowledge.

As you go deeper into meditation you will feel the essence and see how it connects all life to the Great Spirit. As you go deeper still, leaving behind your thoughts and aspirations, all bodily sensations will disappear as you merge into Oneness. You will experience complete peace and a vista of colours expanding before you, culminating in a feeling of bliss.

If you remain silent you will be in the moment, the now, where time stands still and you will feel that you have found the secret of life, the essence that you are. Eventually your mind returns and you are back to your normal consciousness, but with a difference as you now know you can return to that state at any time, for you will have experienced Oneness with God and all life.

Few people understand what is within the earth. They take various readings by drilling and other means; they know that the levels of the rock, the layers, all change. They know through volcanoes and earthquakes how this all changes as one goes deeper towards the core of the earth where, in the very centre, you have a searing heat of tremendous temperature.

Who, among the scientists seeking answers, is looking for the spiritual aspect of the inside of the earth? It probably doesn't cross their minds, but for you, who know that spirit is within all life, then it does not come as a surprise to know that there is spirit within the earth. In fact, you must already be aware, but perhaps hadn't thought of the implications, of the spirit within your earth. Just as your bodies would not work without the presence of spirit, so the earth would be a dead planet without it.

Looking at the physical manifestations before your eyes, or through telescopes, you get some idea of the planets and stars around you. All contain energy, so where does the energy come from, where do the winds come from? We know the tides change and bring winds, but you also hear of the trade winds, even the absence of wind. There is always change on your earth as with all physical manifestations.

All the planets revolve around the sun; all solar systems and galaxies revolve around something greater, so there is movement in all that you can see. It may appear still, as you may feel still at this moment, even though the earth is travelling so fast; but with spirit, the spirit within, the Great Spirit, there is just stillness. There is deep, deep peace, there is deep silence and, yet, it opens up into a vista of wonder.

We have mentioned Oneness, and you may have touched on it from time to time. When on earth we each experienced it in our own way. With today's pressures we understand how difficult it is for you to be at peace, but the treasures received by being at One are many. However, to know it, welcome it and feel it is another matter. When you can accept that all is One and invite the Great Spirit in – although He is, of course, within you – you are halfway to being and experiencing Oneness.

As you go through your lives take time, even in a busy day, to go within. Let yourself go into that feeling, open your hearts and minds to the mysteries of spirit. If you are on a fixed project with time constraints it will help if you stand back just for a moment and then, as you resume your work, you will find that you are recharged and you will receive help in whatever you are doing.

You all have problems in one form or another but, as we have said many times, that is the way you learn on earth and is one of the purposes of incarnation. If everything went smoothly how would you develop your inner being? Why would you need to enquire and where would you enquire?

Spirit, we repeat, is still, but you will feel movement until you have pierced the very essence of spirit and when you reach the core of spirit you will feel such bliss. You will have a knowing beyond anything you have experienced before.

Chapter Six

Inner Realms

We wish to take you on a journey to the Himalayas. Many of you will have lived there in previous lives, but your memory of this has temporarily disappeared while you are in your present bodies. There are many temples high up in the mountains, some that are unknown to man; by unknown to man we mean not recorded and not generally discovered. These are special temples which exist for those who are in a halfway state of living on the earth and halfway living with the angels. You may find this hard to believe, but we assure you that this is correct.

We take you with us high in the atmosphere where the air is less dense, but where your souls have a better connection with All That Is through the Masters on our side of life who are always ready to assist mankind. They appear before those who are lucky enough to be in these temples. We call them temples of light, for they appear to us like large searchlights except that with a searchlight the light goes straight, whereas this light comes out in an ever-expanding ball covering everything within reach.

The peace within the temple is unlike anything you would have experienced on earth. It is so deep that you are still in the silence even if something making a noise is taking place outside. You will not hear it when you are in one of these temples. It is like going deep within your own souls only many, many times deeper and fulfilling. You do not need to speak, or even think, for you are surrounded with the presence of the Great Spirit. You can, however, think of those Masters and they will come and talk to you. They will appear as glowing lights and their proximity will be felt as a beautiful warmth and light within you.

We have said that these temples are unknown to the majority; those who are aware of them will have earned the experience. It is also possible for other people to experience these temples for themselves when they are in deep meditation. Should you be given this opportunity embrace it, for it is a rare privilege granted to those on earth.

We invite you on a journey, a journey of the soul, for the soul is that part of you which, like the human body, encases the spirit. Of course, the soul cannot be seen, it is not physical, but it contains everything about you: knowledge of all your lives, knowledge of all your wishes, of your happiness, of your sadness but, above all, it contains the history of your journey and the pathway that is ahead of you.

On our journey today, we travel above the earth. We take you through the planets and deep, deep, into space, far deeper than man has ever seen with his telescopes. What can possibly be beyond the vision of those telescopes; what indeed? The overriding power there is love and what you see is not individual planets and suns but a wonderful picture, a picture of Oneness.

Oneness contains all the colours known to you, and so many other hues which are known to us. You are in the far reaches of the universe and what you feel at this time is a deep, deep, love. You also feel that you have expanded your inner self and can touch those colours; you feel as though you are the colours. You now see mists which lead you beyond into a vastness you have never experienced. You are right in the middle of the space that *is* the universe.

People do not understand what the universe is. They naturally think that because it is physical there is an end to it. In fact, it is physical and spiritual and, as such, there is no end to it; it just goes on and on into infinity. It becomes more beautiful as you go further in and what is happening is that you are going further and further into God's space.

Relax, let yourself take in the surroundings. The universe is still forming, and you are now in the frontiers that make more stars. Moreover, you are seeing the intelligence of life and the way you perceive intelligence is different from how you view physical things. You feel it, rather than see it, and as you open yourself further there is now a warmth and that is a feeling you have not had before. It is more than what is happening; it is more than bliss, it just *is*. It is the intelligence of all life and you are in its centre.

Rest awhile; absorb everything around you. You are taking in not physical matter but that which came before physical matter, that which forms physical matter. You are taking in the origins of life. As you are silent, for a moment or two allow yourself to explore the feeling, let it come into the very centre of your being. You see what appears like the edge of a sun; let it come into you for it is giving you light and strength.

Before we move on let yourself feel completely free; let yourself feel as though you are flying. You are flying without any limits and, yes, you can begin to see the twinkling of the stars ahead, for you are returning to that part of the universe you feel you know. As you come back through all the planets and return to your body we hope that you have enjoyed this special time and trust that you will retain the feelings you have experienced.

It is with pleasure and love that we come to you this morning and bring greetings from a world of which your soul is aware but is currently unknown to you. It is a world full of music, love and peace; an enchanting world where, being on a higher vibration, anything can occur. The music and colours are, literally, out of your world, beyond anything you could imagine. The music has a tone all of its own. The sky and the grass, comparable to that of earth, merge in light. The light itself is bright, so bright that unless one is used to it one cannot see anything.

This is what awaits when you complete a life of service, when you do unto others what you would have them do unto you. A life when you think of what you can do for others, when you are cheery, when you make people laugh, when you heal the sick, when you comfort the bereaved. When you have lived the teachings of the Lord Jesus and it is time for you to return to the next world you will find yourself in surroundings similar to those described.

However, you can have heaven on earth, for as you sit in comfort with your heart and soul open to All That Is you have within a beauty all of its own, that you can feel and almost touch. You do not have to wait to cross to our side of life to enjoy these conditions. It is a matter of becoming and staying close to your real self, finding your God within, for God is everyone's God because there is only One. When you are close to your God you *are* the One.

As you let yourself go, as you open to All That Is, as you leave the little self behind, you will become the whole. It will feel as though you are the One and, as long as you don't think back to the little self, you will retain this Oneness, for the Oneness is the natural *being* within you all. You feel as you have never felt before; you have an explosion of light, of love, of peace, and you find the truth within.

We wish to speak of places as yet unknown to you. You are being taken to one of these areas in the celestial regions; do not think of the physical for you will be distracted in understanding where you are. You are in the spirit and angel realms; this region is made up of undiluted love, where an expression of feeling and movement from within takes place.

There is a purple hue all around, and a feeling of upliftment as you experience a deeper extension into purity. It is like a soft bed of rose petals, with the perfume becoming stronger as you enter the chamber which is embossed with warm light. A path, ready for you to follow, now appears. The light is even brighter; there is a suggestion of being lifted up higher and higher until there is no feeling or touch, leading on to an internal expression of peace; deep, deep peace.

The road levels out and there are a thousand mingling bright colours: colours beyond the mind's understanding, beyond description and, yet, a feeling of being at home, being at the centre of everything, being in the womb ready to explore the greatness all around. There is a pulsating rhythm of space-like waves of different pure colours and this opens up into a carpet of the finest grass you could imagine. As you walk tenderly on this grass you await the opening of a large door in front of you. You wait patiently and, little by little, the door opens and you are in the most amazing garden with plants of different sizes and colours, all growing in perfect response to the Creator.

Each plant gives out a welcoming light and perfume and as you walk through the garden there is a light above you, a strong sun-like light, which is beckoning you ever forward. As further doors open, you feel full to the brim with knowledge, with wisdom, with peace, and you feel the truth within as your whole being reverberates in bliss. You are at One with all creation and you *are* the Creator. You can do anything you desire, but you are in awe of this power, this beauty, this stillness, this silence which contains everything. You feel as though you merge with all life and, within, it seems the experience will last forever.

Now, something is slowly bringing you back through all the different layers of spirit: back, back into your world, into your physical world, where you are aware of your body, of touch. You feel you have been on the most wonderful journey. You are at perfect peace and you have a warmth inside which sustains your feeling of complete Oneness.

There is a feeling of being lifted up into an in-between land, between spirit and earth, and although it seems to be 'up there' it is, in fact, in the same space, for we are all in the same space; it is just that we vibrate at different rates. There are angels all around and, in this loving space, the light is so bright that one cannot see beyond the immediate surroundings. Here, the presence of many loved ones, and those who have progressed much further, is felt.

They are now showing the special rooms where walls appear in different colours and, yet, are not solid although they appear so. They are all illuminated, for the buildings themselves, although simple, have wonderful architecture. This is the supreme thought-world where anything can happen. It is where one aspires to be when in the spirit world. There are those beings who are only too delighted to show you where they spend their working lives, for to sit back and do nothing is certainly not encouraged.

Within the soul there is a need to look forward, to aim higher and, therefore, it is necessary to work in one way or another. It can be simply cleaning, it can be creating, it can be painting; it can be all manner of things, but when it comes from the heart there is progression. So, in this beautiful building there is a feeling of achievement. To reach such heights one has spent many lives of service, creating feelings of love and thought for others.

In the process one does not need to think of oneself as everything is taken care of, for as you give so you receive. In accord with natural law one receives much more than one gives; natural law is not only for the earth but for all life, wherever it may be. It could be another planet, it may be another universe, or in the spirit world, but wherever God is, wherever His people are, then there is natural law which is completely fair and just. There is no question about it, and there does not need to be, because the word natural explains everything. When you are in a different dimension all will still feel natural.

It is a pleasure to visit this area which is a halfway place, a halfway situation, and, yet, it is more than halfway. To those who have not reached it, it is the ultimate, but to us it is still only the halfway stage.

As one moves on to different lives, different understandings, you will forever be seeking more knowledge, more wisdom, more light and there is never a stage when you will be completely satisfied. There will always be the need to learn and experience more.

This is a glimpse into the future and remember that when you are serving your fellow man you can always go within to re-visit and experience such places.

There is before you a mountain with stepping stones: an easy way to climb. As you climb up the mountain a beautiful mauve colour appears, going deeper into purple as you rise above any height you have ever before ascended.

As you go up, and up and up, take in the love that is here; take in the beauty, for you are now looking down on your earth. See how beautiful it appears from space.

You, for this is your spiritual self, continue to climb and, as you continue ever upwards, you feel yourself becoming lighter. Any aches or pains disappear for you are climbing, climbing into the love spheres of spirit.

As you climb even higher, you lose all thoughts of self as you come into a special area where the light is purer, pure white, almost invisible and, yet, dazzling.

You are now with the Masters; you may or may not see them, but you feel them. You sense that they are here; you are within their auras and, as you open your heart, you start to feel at One with them. You feel enfolded in a circle of love, a circle of peace and a stillness never before experienced.

Enjoy these moments as the Masters give you their blessings, and as you stay awhile longer in their presence you receive within knowledge, wisdom and love.

Slowly, you return to your physical body to enjoy the peace that now surrounds you.

Chapter Seven

Experiencing Sai Baba

'It gives me much joy to be with you today. As you know I had the privilege of travelling the world and speaking to various groups when on earth. I have not been back in the spirit world for very long, but long enough to have met many of those you know, or did know, when on earth. I have not lost any of my earthly attributes: in fact, I have received more because the Great Spirit is able to expand my being, expand my knowledge, and expand my work which is now talking to people on earth in this way. I am talking to you in a general manner, for there is much work to be done.

'My spiritual focus on the earth was, as you know, with the Avatar, Sathya Sai Baba. Since I have returned to spirit I have seen Him in all His glory. I cannot begin to describe the vision, or the feelings that came with it. Suffice to say that I was engulfed in golden light with a love that is beyond description. I was taken up into the highest heaven and stayed there, from your time perspective, many hours. My whole being has changed, has been uplifted, and I speak with such joy and friendliness, compassion, and love for all people. The experience has left me empowered with light and love.

'I am, therefore, obliged to share with you, and as many as possible, the wonder of spirit from the spirit within each individual to the Great Spirit, the Godhead. Once you have experienced the Godhead at first hand your life will never be the same. I am able to be anywhere at any time; I go where it is felt that I am needed and I bring the love of the Father to all who are in my vision.

'I cannot explain how fortunate you and those who receive these words are for they are not only receiving the words, they are also receiving the love and light of the Father. The compassion that is embodied within all life shows itself so much when people give themselves in service. The secret of life is giving, giving, giving, giving of yourselves, helping when you can and giving money, if it is appropriate, but it is the actions of giving that are the most important. There is much work to be done on the earth and it is by people giving of themselves as *love in action* that will change the world. It has been said that the Golden Age is within everyone. Of course, it is; it is the God Spirit. The God Spirit *is* the Golden Age, so, as you come more and more into His Spirit you will bring the Golden Age into not only your lives but to the lives of all the people you meet.

'I had amazing experiences when on earth: I went to many countries, I spent time with more than one guru, but my time with Sai Baba was beyond description. Where I am now we do not need to talk of individual spirit people, for all is One. However, with my experiences on earth and now in spirit I can assure you that the Great Spirit is waiting and willing to be with you in His fullness so that you may receive the same as I have.'

'My dear friends; we have such memories together. You helped me in more ways than you realise. I know I was quite a strong spokesperson in many ways, but I am sure you appreciated I was coming from love. I was coming from that Great One we followed, Sai Baba.

'We believed He was God. He used to say "I am God and so are you", but we couldn't accept it. We accepted the words, of course, and we sang the words: beautiful songs. We could see God in what He did, in what He taught, in what He was like to be with, for I, in company with Richard (the Channel), had the most wonderful experiences in His presence. That stays with me and I know it stays with Richard.

'I hope that we were able to relate His love when we came back from India and talked to the groups, for we felt as though God's love was shining in our faces. We organised large public meetings and invited guests who gave talks, and we sang. We experienced that special feeling and His presence was palpable to all who were open enough to receive.

'When you cast your minds back to how you felt in those times think what it must be like here where we are closer to the God Spirit, when we are able to feel that love continuously, for we do have contact with the Masters. We feel as though we are them when we are in their presence. So, when Sai Baba said, "I am God and so are you" believe it, for it is true. The problem for you on earth is that, in your physical bodies, you are surrounded by material things and you cannot normally accept this truth, except when you are in meditation, and with the feeling you have now when love is flowing out of you, is flowing into you, and is all around you.

'To come back to those wonderful days, people gave me credit for so much of it. It was not me, dear friends, it was all of you and, above that, it was Sai Baba; then we knew that things were always perfect. The time went by so quickly and you now only have memories of the amazing experiences we had, but you can relive those experiences now while you are still in the physical body when you go deeply inside.

'So, thank you my dearest friends. My love for you is endless.'

'The Channel and I remember being together in this room many times. We talked at length about spirit; we talked at length about the Great One in India (Sai Baba). In fact, I was privileged to speak there at Christmas for so many years and I was blessed to be given that opportunity. I enjoyed every moment, as I did when I came to your great country, and I met so many wonderful people in my life on earth.

'I also experimented with different religious and spiritual avenues, but I always came back to that Great One in India. He used to tell me to go and experiment, knowing that I would always come back to His feet. He used to say it was not necessary to see Him, not necessary to worship the body, for it is misguided to worship the body as the body is only a vehicle for spirit; far more important to worship the God within.

'In my later life I travelled the world. I had so many wonderful experiences, but I was always led on by the inner being of which you speak. I can assure you that this is the best way to live your life, to be in constant touch with your God within, for He will take you where you need to go. He will protect you, He will guard you, He will guide you. He will bring you to such heights in your life that you will experience from within all that you could possibly desire.

'I had my failings; there is no-one on earth who does not but, overall, my life on earth was so wonderful that I have taken all those experiences and brought them with me to spirit. From here I am helping many who wish to have the knowledge that I've been given. Not only am I helping people on my side of life, but I am glad to say that I work with many on the earth.

'I like your humour: life should be founded on humour, for that is why God invented it. One of the gifts you on earth and those of us in spirit have, and will always have, is that you can always laugh at something when things are not going very well; the best advice is to laugh at yourself.

'Well, I hope I've brought a little laughter to your meeting today. I have enjoyed being with you; it has brought back old times. Most of those who used to meet here are now with me in spirit, but we keep an eye on all of you and all who need any help in whatever direction. I feel Oneness with you all.'

You have been blessed tonight to see and taste vibhuti, which has been produced by the Lord for His devotees and others who come to hear of Sai Baba. When He was on the earth there were many millions of devotees around the world, but very few of them lived the life completely that His teachings required of them. Nevertheless, His words and His teachings have spread even further. Now, Sai Baba is talking and teaching again at Muddenahalli, India, in His subtle body and through a former student, especially chosen for the purpose.

This has caused upset with many traditional devotees who believe Sai Baba would not talk through anyone other than Himself. However, in His subtle body, schools and hospitals with free care continue to be built, for His physical incarnation has not yet been completely fulfilled.

You are, therefore, privileged to be hearing about Him and tasting vibhuti which has been manifested out of thin air. Sai Baba has created many miracles, but the greatest is bringing pure love into people's hearts and transforming them so that they, in turn, will help others. The time is coming when Prema Sai (the third incarnation) will be here, announcing Himself while most of you are still alive. You are privileged to have this news, for it will be the start of a worldwide transformation of people from within.

Remember that you received these words and know that this will happen. There are already many devotees but many, many, many more will be required to be spokesmen and women in this New Age. Sai Baba's mission has been taking place for over half a century and, in time to come, there will be a huge increase in the number of people who become aware of Him.

So, we say to you, take the love that has come with this holy ash. Feel it within you; it will not only heal you it will give you strength, courage, fortitude and confidence in yourselves, a confidence that is within, that will drive you forward on your individual pathways as you all link into the wonderful future that is ahead of you.

Note: After leaving His physical body in 2011, Sai Baba immediately began appearing in His subtle form, or light body, to selected individuals. In May 2014 He made it publicly known that He was continuing His mission of service and transformation of humanity on a worldwide scale.

P rior to the weekly circle meeting, Richard (the Channel) related this remarkable experience.

'On Monday, 6th February 2017, I noticed a deep scratch on the rear door on the driver's side of my car. It appeared that someone had used a screwdriver or penknife in an act of vandalism. I was quite annoyed as the car was less than one year old and otherwise in perfect condition. Fortunately, I showed my neighbour the mark and touched it to discover it had gone through the paint and onto the steel.

'That evening I attended a circle meeting in Bristol, taking with me vibhuti which had been materialised in India and this was sampled by those present. I also channelled a talk about Sai Baba, now in His subtle body.

'Upon returning home I noted that the mark on the car was still evident. The next morning, I went out early to the shops and, upon my return, again looked for the mark on the door. Imagine my surprise when I couldn't find it. I fetched a cloth and cleaned the area thoroughly, but the paintwork was like new again with no marks or scratches on the door!'

'You have heard Richard describe his experience earlier today. We confirm that every word is true, and you would have loved to see the expression on his face; disbelief, incredulity. There is more happening in your world now of this nature than you would imagine and there is so much more to come.

'Be close to your God as you go through life, feel His Spirit guiding you and you, too, could have experiences that logically should not happen and are, literally, beyond the physics of your world. From our world nothing is impossible, for we can mingle between the metals, the vibrations and the atoms and we can vary substances, but this can only be done with the grace of God.

'You have heard of the miracles performed by the Great Ones who have lived on earth. God can do anything and when one feels in accord physically, mentally and spiritually within, surrendering to that force as a partner to it, then anything is possible. It is through the grace of God that this power can be used by one in such a close state with the Great Spirit but there has to be a good reason, a reason for good, to uplift people, to bring them into the understanding themselves.

'So, we are pleased this incident occurred and are happy that you are aware of it. Therefore, you will be open to anything that may happen in the future.'

'You described Me so eloquently the last time you were all together. You saw Me in my orange gown and I have come again today because I feel your love and welcome is so great that I am attracted to your circle.

'I want to say that the world is not quite ready to hear My words, for they have heard them over many, many, years, but how many have put them into practice? You could count on the fingers of one hand those who live their whole life according to My teachings. Nevertheless, many have spread the words that I have given; many have spread My teachings and told of My actions.

'Many have told of the free hospitals that I built, of the water projects that I instigated and soon there will be another who will continue My work. In the meantime, it is down to people like you who are ready to absorb My teachings, to spread the word, not necessarily using My name but by spreading the teachings that I stand for. The values, the five human values that life should be based on are: love, peace, truth, right conduct and non-violence. People should know that there is no death. People should know that all life is One.'

I AM.
I AM in the wind.
I AM in the sea.
I AM in every little raindrop.
I AM in the air you breathe.
I AM above you, below you, around you and within you.
There is nowhere that I AM not.

'You will speak the words of truth, you will speak the words of peace, of love, of right conduct and of non-violence, for the world needs these values more today than it ever has. Above all, it is by example that people will come to understand and want to know more about spiritual teachings; more about ancient wisdom, about real love, spiritual love, the love that is all around you, that is you, that is the real you. The love that knows no equal contains everything; it contains beauty, it contains freshness, newness.

'So, when you feel that love within know that it comes from your Creator and when you link into that love you are linking into Me and all as One.'

The following extracts have been compiled from my meetings in Russia (See page 72 Chapter 1). I also give, verbatim, words channelled directly from Sai Baba.

'As you come together in love we join you, bringing love from the next dimension and we invite you to open your hearts to us; we are not far away at all. You tend to look upwards to seek your loved ones who are with us, but we are virtually in the same space as you; it is just that the frequency, the dimension, is different. If you were able to raise your consciousness you would be able to see us and talk to us, but you are on the earth for a special journey.'

'All people who take birth on the earth do so by request and there are always many, many, queueing up for it. It is the most important spiritual growing time when one spends a life on earth. It is like the university of life and it is a place where only certain experiences can be received, so people value life on earth. A plan is agreed before incarnation and everything is wiped from one's memory beforehand, so you have no recollection of why you have come to the earth. Neither do you remember your past lives, for the simple reason that if you knew them your experience on earth would not be so valuable. You are seeking to find your pathway. You may go down side roads, you may be distracted, but that does not matter for all experiences are important.'

'Eventually, you will be led back to your pathway, your reason for this life. You may wonder what the reason is; some of you may know why you are here. The main reason, of course, is to find your real self and to be love itself; to give love to all you meet, to serve, to help your fellow men and women. We know that when one is happy, when one looks forward, when one looks to God, when one is full of confidence and happiness, a beautiful life will take place.'

'You have joy in your lives but, at the same time, you also have the most difficult times when your loved ones have departed this life. We hasten to tell you that they have not gone very far and they hear you when you speak to them. We encourage you all to do so, just as we encourage you to talk to Sai Baba or whoever you call your God. He has said He wants to be your friend, but you naturally look up to Him because of His incalculable intelligence. Sai Baba has said you try to understand Him but how can you understand Him?'

> I am all things and all mysteries. I am beyond understanding and yet, I have told you, I am in you and you are in Me. When you believe this, when you live your life according to this understanding, you will become closer to Me and I can help you as I'm helping all people at all times. I have no favourites, I am just love. My totality is love. Therefore, when you come to Me, when you touch Me you are touching the greatest thing on earth and in the heavens, and that is pure unconditional love. As you progress in your life, as you help others, as you think of what you can do in a situation to help, when you physically help someone, when you pray to be used in service, you will receive all the help you need.
>
> As you look inwardly you will find Me within you because that is where I am. I am in every cell, I am in every atom, but the biggest place I am is in your heart, your spiritual heart. As you feel Me within, which you can do at this moment for there is warmth surrounding your heart, there is a special feeling in all of you. As you concentrate within on Me, on love as you see it, real love, then your true self, which is Me, will come to the fore, will come to the front of your life.
>
> Your life will be expanded, you will see much more clearly, and you will know what to do. You will feel happy for My main message is *be happy* and when you are in a state of happiness your whole body, all the cells in your body are raised, and your health will improve. You all have to go through certain situations which may involve bad health, but the more you live your life in service to others the more this will help you to overcome all your problems.

'You spoke about Me earlier. You talked about the things I manifested; you talked about the games I play. Well, *you* think I play games. I don't play games; everything is in My hand. I can will anything, but I like to make you feel good. I like to make you realise there is so much more to life than you have seen, that you think about.

'I have given many gifts to people. I will give the gift of love, the spiritual gifts, for that is what I am here for. I will give gifts to all who give to others and I will help all along their chosen road. When they are working for the good of mankind then I will bring them gifts that they have never dreamed of; gifts of the Spirit.

'I used to produce physical gifts, but that was only to attract people, and a great many misread My deeds for they thought that by receiving a physical gift from Me they were the chosen ones; far from it. Those who did not receive physical gifts, but received spiritual gifts, are the ones, the chosen ones, and there are so many in the world today that are ready to be chosen. They are ready for the work to be done.

'I may not be here physically, but I am here always. I have always been and I always will be. People heard of Me far and wide. They will hear of Me with a different name in the days to come and they will hear, all nations will hear of Me, but you will hear before most of them for I am to come again. I will appear in that wonderful eastern country that is so well-known, where I was born before, where all the great Avatars have been born. You don't need to see the physical person, you have Me with you whenever you need Me.'

'Be aware of Me and you will find your life will be transformed. You will see Me in all the little events of life, you will see Me in the large events of life; you will see Me in everything.

'Take this feeling, this awareness, with you every second of the day: when you are preparing food, eating it and cleaning the dishes afterwards.

'Be aware of Me in your silent moments and your noisy moments, when in discussion and laughter with others. Be aware of Me when you are reading, when you are playing and when you are working; and especially when you are serving.

'You know I am with you always but the knowledge and practical awareness of this takes you into a different dimension. Of course, you will still be living on the earth, but mentally and spiritually you will be walking on air, on water.

'So, as you go through life, be aware of Me at all times for I am you and you are Me. What could be simpler!'

Chapter Eight

Meditation

When one is able to sit quietly in the early hours there is peace, tangible peace, all around and it is a perfect time for meditation, before the distractions of the day. The mind, of course, is still active and can easily override the peace and Oneness. Overcoming the mind's excursions is a continual discipline which should become easier the more one meditates. However, the mind or the ego, for they are closely linked, linger in the background of one's life ever eager to come to the forefront and raise many questions and doubts.

The process of meditation, where ego is forgotten, leads one to creative, compassionate and loving thoughts. Opening oneself to the Great Spirit continues this train of thought, leading to real meditation and, without thinking, a feeling of Oneness. It is in this state that real spiritual progress is made as one's own spirit comes to the forefront of the whole being and remains there long after the meditation period has finished.

From mind or ego domination one is transformed into a spirit-led state where communion with the Great Spirit is made. The body and mind are both relaxed, leaving the real self to take over and replace the thought process of the mind. In this state, a peace beyond understanding arises and leads to a feeling of unconditional love and bliss where all the cells of the body feel alive. There is a tingling and expectation of beautiful Oneness where time and all bodily awareness is forgotten. One's heart centre is warm and expanding and the whole being is now ready to receive wisdom and pro-active ideas in the evolving process of life.

As one reluctantly returns to a normal conscious state the body feels rejuvenated and ready for the adventure of the day ahead, where one can take the recently experienced peace and unconditional love. It can be likened to a light leading one through the rest of the day with heart and body uplifted. Challenges are met with a will and a new-found confidence, resulting in a successful and satisfying day at work and play.

I AM with you now and always.

I AM in the leaf of the tree, in the blade of grass, the tiny droplet of water, the snowflake, the white frost.

I AM in the mist, in the cloud, in the very atmosphere of the earth.

I AM.

Feel Me, feel Me in your most inner being, for I AM in all of you, every cell, every atom.

I know you as a friend. I have known you since the beginning of time because I AM you, and you are Me.

You are now opening up within yourself and a feeling of consciousness is taking over; first your heart area, then your head, then your middle body, arms and legs. Overall, this feeling, this openness, this love, this connection, is going beyond your body and is all around you, ever-expanding in the room. You are filled with love; you sit in peace and receive the bounty of the Spirit. You feel Oneness: all thoughts leave you other than your connection with All That Is, for you feel you *are* All That Is.

Take this love experience, this Oneness, into your day. Remember all you meet contain the Spirit of God and they are inherently at One with you and with all life. You are already connected to us when you sit and talk to people and, although they may not realise it, you will be connected at the heart of *their* being. So, somewhere within they will recognise and be touched by God's love emanating from your spirit.

Think of this wonderful connection when you make your way through your day and you will find that you will be uplifted within. Whatever you do, whomever you meet, through contact, by whatever means, you will feel their heart and soul within you.

So, be aware and remember who you really are for this connection of love is inherent within you.

I AM already in your heart.
I AM with you now and always.
I AM in your soul.
I AM your Spirit.
I AM all you need.

Call on Me and, together, we will change the world: not by any specific action, but by you and all those who give their love to Me and all life.

When you open up your inner being you will open like a flower and as you help those around you that love, healing, companionship and communion will spread from your neighbourhood and, together, we *will* change the world.

As you sit in silence, opening your spiritual heart to All That Is, you receive the love of spirit. That love is all around you, is within you, is you; for at the heart of your spirit is love.

You are spirit encasing a human body so as you go inwards, to your very soul, you will take in the purity of God's Spirit. At the same time, through love, your channels of communication are opened. You cannot hold onto love, for love is an energy which requires movement and the more that you send love out and think of others the more you, yourself, receive. This is the law of abundance: the more that you give of yourself, whether material or spiritual, the more you will receive. There is a catch, of course, because if you are doing it to receive then it will not work, for you will have put a condition on your giving.

Giving, like love, should be unconditional, for love originates from the Great Spirit and His love cannot be other than unconditional. The Great Spirit knows only how to give. He does not need to receive for He is the Creator and He has created movement in all life. At the heart of Spirit, the nucleus, there is stillness, peace beyond comprehension, but all around there is movement. There is continuous movement in the universe and on the earth.

As you sit in meditation you can reach the nucleus, the centre of all life, and when you find that centre your whole world will appear to stop as you gradually become at One with God. You become One with the Great Spirit of all life and it is here that you will receive the bounty of Spirit. Your mind will become still, as there is no need for thought in the heaven that you have entered.

I AM.
I AM in the gentlest breeze.
I AM in the largest gust of wind.
I AM in the little drop of rain.
I AM in the hail.
I AM the snowflake.
I AM the frost that greets you on a winter's morning.
I AM the fresh air you breathe each morning.
I AM the water you drink.
I AM the air you breathe.
I AM the space within you and all around you.
I AM the flower, your favourite flowers.
I AM everywhere.
There is nowhere I AM not, but where do *you* find Me?

You find Me when you lose yourself in happiness, in concentration on the beauties of life, in fun, in hard work, in day-to-day little jobs, in large projects.

You find Me everywhere and at all times, but very few are aware of Me, even those who say they know Me. How can anyone know Me?

Even they forget: they start each day with a promise to be close to Me and aware of Me, but once the day starts and they become involved in other things they forget where I AM.

I never forget, for if I did you would not be here.
I AM.
I AM you.
I AM the ground you stand on.
I AM the chair you sit on.
I AM the world you live in.
I AM the universe.
I love you.

I love you as a son and daughter, as a husband and wife, but I love you as God for you are the same as Me.

I AM you and you are Me.

Your hearts are open at this moment and you can feel Me within.

Take this feeling with you; remember and feel Me in all you do, wherever you go.

At any time remember you were given this body to experience.

You were given the knowledge that I AM within and you were given the opportunity to know Me, to feel Me, to be Me.

Take the opportunity, My dear ones.

As you open your whole being to All That Is you are making a statement, an intended statement, showing your love by your attitude as though you were making an offering to your Creator. You are, in fact, sharing in His love for within each one of us all, whether on earth or in spirit, the Lord resides. His Spirit is ageless, intangible, and is everywhere within the physical worlds and in the unseen worlds.

The act of opening to the Great Spirit allows you to become One with Him, knowing He is by your side as you go through life. You can call on Him at any time; you can feel Him as His love spreads throughout your body. You, in turn, pass His love on to all you meet. You may not think you are doing it by just talking to someone, or by a kind acknowledgement or wave, but all these actions contain the love of the Great Spirit.

You will find that the Great Spirit's love that passes through you to others will have a lasting effect on them. Those who know you will want to be in your presence, for they will be attracted to you like a magnet. You may think this gives you a great responsibility, and in a way it does, but you only need to go about your daily tasks as normal and let the Great Spirit do the rest.

It is when you have the opportunity to sit in meditation with the Great Spirit that you can experience His great love as you continue to open up yourself to All That Is. You will be aware of a light, a special silence and peace within which becomes warm, and a tangible joy spreads through you as you stay in the arms of the Great Spirit. You have reached the centre of your life and all life, for you are in that timeless condition where nothing matters, when thoughts disappear and you bathe in the glory of God.

Feel the expansion within, let the love, that beautiful feeling, take over all your being and all that immediately surrounds you. As you stay there, feel the love extending outwards in all directions as you become the centre, the nucleus of all life. The longer you stay with love pouring out of you the longer you will want to stay in the moment, the moment of all moments created by the Great Spirit for you and all life to experience and live in.

Gradually, you become aware of the feeling returning to your body, to your mind. You will know that God is within not only you but everything around you, including the air you breathe. So, as you go through life take love with you, knowing that God will be with you now and always.

I AM the light.
I AM the dark, the dawn and the sunset.
I AM.
I AM the air you breathe.
I AM you, you are Me and together We Are.
I AM the sun, the moon, every twinkle in the sky.
I AM the stars and the space between.
I AM the twinkle in the eye.
I AM your mind and I see what you see.
I AM in your heart.
I AM your heart.
I AM the moment.
I AM the silence.
I AM the embryo for all life.
I AM the newborn baby, the mother and the father.
I AM the newborn chick.
I AM the large white whale.
I AM the water in the ocean.
I AM the ocean.
I AM.
I AM all life and all life is Me.
I AM your laughter.
I AM your crying.
I AM your pleasure.
I AM your sadness.
I AM the nucleus of creation.
I AM the power within creation.
I AM the power that activates all movement in the earth.
I AM the power that activates all movement in the universe.
I AM in you and you are in Me.

As you are in meditation, when all thoughts begin to evaporate, you come to that inner grace, that peace beyond understanding and something pulls you to go deeper. Outside influences are around you, but you manage to keep them at bay as you are in your special place.

Deeper still, and you feel yourself going further inward until you are no longer aware of anything around you except wholeness, a wholeness that is expanding beyond your body. It can be described as 'space' or 'nothingness' but a feeling takes over, a wonderful Oneness. You realise you are still where you were and, yet, you have started on the road to infinity…

You now see images as you continue travelling far within. They are brushed aside and you aim for the centre, on and on, on and on: stillness can now almost be heard. You think you've found the nucleus, but that opens up to further, deeper space.

You stop there as the expansion within you increases: the colours come in and you become aware of your physical surroundings again. You are being pulled back gently, gently, and you are once again aware of your body.

You feel contentment, happiness, joy, and you do not wish to leave, but you know that all your physical awareness has returned. You are then ready to go about your daily life full of peace and love which feels like a song, a perfect melody, within you.

I AM your inner self.

I AM the love within you and all life.

I AM at the very centre of your being and all beings.

Without the I AM there would be no life, no physical life, no spiritual life.

Feel the I AM within.

Experience the I AM expanding within.

Become One with the I AM and you will feel the peace that passes all understanding. You will feel the love that is not only at the centre of all life but is also in the fullness of life.

Once you touch the I AM within, and surrender the little self, you will have an explosion of light and bliss within your whole being. You will feel love expanding beyond your body, beyond the air and space around you and beyond the room you are in as your whole world is filled with the I AM and the experience of Oneness with God.

As you continue to feel expansion all thoughts have left you as you dwell in the moment. The moment feels like the nucleus of All That Is and the nucleus will itself expand as you feel ripples of ecstasy. You are now in the very centre of your God. You are in Him and He is in you. You can stay there forever, for this is your *real* self experiencing through your whole being.

There will come a time when you return to your normal conscious state, the difference being that, once you have experienced the expansion of love within, your life will never be quite the same again. You will have the knowing that God is within you, and at any time you can return to the I AM which is within and all around you. Not only can you return to that experience, but it will remain in the background as you go through your normal life when you meet people, when you are working, when you are playing and when you just *are*.

You will not then have to think or plan but will be guided through life having such a glow within that you will be led to wherever you need to go. You will be fulfilling your life plan and as you serve your fellow man you will have unbelievable pleasure in living the rest of your life at One with All That Is.

As you rest in Me, know that all you ever have been and ever will be is in this *moment*. Treasure the *now* for only the now exists. Whatever you are doing or thinking you are in the now. All your life has led to this moment, the now. The rest of your life does not exist except in this moment.

So, wherever you are, whatever you are doing, whether you are worried, happy or at peace, every thought and attitude can be changed in the now. Spend time in the now; be aware only of the moment and you will begin the rest of your life in love, for in the moment, in the now, creation first began and, in the moment, creation continues.

Whatever your life has been, with all its multitude of experiences, everything began in the moment. A new career can be started in the moment, new thought patterns, new relationships but, above all, being at One with All That Is, in the moment, is the ultimate experience.

You can be at One in the body, as you lose your awareness of it, by being in the moment. Inside you feel warmth, unconditional love, peace beyond description and are now only conscious of the heaven within you.

I AM here.
I AM with you always.
I AM your heart.
I AM love.
I AM All That Is.
I surround you.
I AM in you.
I AM you.
I AM in all life.
I AM in the air you breathe.
I AM in the rain; I AM in each tiny droplet.
I AM the sunshine; the rays that penetrate the atmosphere.
I AM the trees you see, the leaves that form in Spring and fall in Autumn.
I AM the energy within the tree.
I AM the energy within you.
I AM your friend.
I AM here for you to lean on at any time.
I AM here to guide you, to guard you.
I AM here to wipe away your tears of sadness.
I AM here to enjoy your tears of happiness.
I AM closer to you than you are to yourself.
I knock on your door and await your reply.
I sing to you like a bird.
I sing to you through melodious voices.
I provide everything you need.
I wait for you to respond.
I wait as you experience life to the full.
I wait on you for I AM you.
I love you and I AM One with you.
I AM there when you awake and blossom as a flower.
I wait as you become One with Me.
I AM you and you are Me.

Chapter Nine

Oneness

We wish to say a few words about the Oneness of all life, or nonduality as certain people on your earth describe it. Many centuries ago there was an understanding among spiritual people from the East, which followed the ancient wisdom handed down, teaching that all life was One and that mankind, the animal kingdom and all life, wherever it might be, was One and connected.

Many books have been written on the subject. Apart from those originating in the East, which can be difficult to understand, there has grown up in the Western world a desire by some people to read about nonduality. It is considered by some to be the utopia of life and that there is nothing else to learn. Some people describe nonduality very simply and say that life has no problems for those who are awakened. This is not strictly true, for all people will naturally have problems as they go through their life. However, when people are awakened they still meet problems, but because of their thinking, their understanding, they don't regard them as obstacles and deal with them without too much trouble.

Now, the word 'awakened' has many connotations. You could say that you were awakened when you first knew there was more to life than the physical. You could say that you were awakened when you knew that there was a God. You could say that you were awakened when you first discovered a particular teaching or belief which resonated within you.

There are very few people who are truly awakened. We would describe them as Masters, like the living Jesus, the Christ. These Masters are, indeed, open to all life and they not only know what is happening in other people's lives they are also able to transmute one physical thing into another. The real Masters, of course, only do this for good and it is a rare privilege to be in the presence of such a Master.

To return to the word 'nonduality'. Some people go to great lengths to describe nonduality and confuse the reader or listener. Others make it sound so simple that people cannot believe it to be true. As always there is a middle road, but what is often missing or overlooked is the love of the Great Spirit, for without that love, without the One God, there would be no nonduality; there would be nothing.

So, in considering awakening and nonduality, we feel this should be discussed and taught with one great thought behind it: the love of God. The understanding of nonduality is certainly a great step forward in one's spiritual life, but do not for one moment think that it is the end. It is only the start.

Nevertheless, when investigation is taken upon oneself, recognising the love of God, a great foundation will have been formed within and one will have such an advantage with that understanding.

We often talk about being at One, but do you know what being at One really is, for there is only the Great Spirit. God is not at One for He is *the* One, and He is in all of you and you are in Him. It sounds simple to be at One when you just open yourselves to Him, but it is more than just a feeling. It is a presence; it is His presence within you that you are able to perceive, that you are able to know is there and, when you do feel His presence, you are halfway to being at One with God and all life.

As you notice feelings within your heart area let yourselves go, let Him be noticeable within you, for He is within you and He is only waiting for you to know it, to know that His Spirit is within every part of you and within every part of everyone. It is within all things, including the air you breathe, and the heat from the sun; even a clod of earth contains so much life.

So, take it further and think about the life, *real life*, that is within you. Can you imagine how much is really there?

The Channel is receiving these words because we are all One; we are all connected. Something happening in the here and now can be felt inwardly on the other side of the earth and can also be felt on our side of life. Every cell, every atom, has that spark of the Great Spirit and is interconnected. For instance, you may wonder why somebody suddenly begins to enquire about spiritual matters. This is because all information exists within the individual; it just needs a prompt to set it in motion. It may be something quite innocuous, or the bodily death of a friend or family member, an accident, an illness or chance meeting. There are so many reasons.

The concept that we are all One is not accepted by most people. There is an element of fear perpetrated by the ego; one subtle ramification is that it, the little self, will cease to exist should one attain complete understanding and surrender into the Oneness of all life. The ego is a very strong force in one's life and has been given to you by the Great Spirit for a purpose. As you grow up and lead your lives you need both strength and ego to propel you through the rigours and problems it presents. Some people seem to have an extreme of ego, whereas others have only a little, but as one moves toward nonduality, or Oneness, then the ego will gradually disappear.

People say they believe in the Oneness of all life, yet wonder what would happen to them should they let go completely. The answer is that life would be no different because the feeling within would be magnified, would take in the whole world, the whole universe, but you would still have the drive that the ego gives you. The little me would disappear and you would have in its place the whole world, all of life. Can you imagine?

The next time you experience that Oneness in the now, try to forget the me part of you; then open up and stay open to All That Is. You will gradually find the ego disappearing and being replaced by the most wonderful feeling within, where anything is achievable and where your whole world is as One.

Everyone and everything is spirit. All are linked together in God's Spirit, so to accept the enormity of the meaning of Oneness takes time for some people to accept. Some pooh-pooh it; a rare few have an amazing experience where they go into a wonderful state of being when they no longer feel their individuality. They literally become One with All That Is. They become One with their brothers and sisters, and One with their enemies, for in that state friends and enemies are the same because, if there is only One, how can there be any difference? There cannot be.

People have brief experiences of Oneness; others, like the Masters, feel at One permanently. We are not suggesting that you spend your life trying to be at One, for trying is not the way. The answer is to let go, let go of the mind and all the thousands of thoughts that are around you.

Go inside and discover your real self. It is not physical, it is merely a feeling within which will gradually increase as it grows and, eventually, you will experience your whole self expanding in Oneness. In this heightened state you will appear to be in the centre of the room and then spreading to fill the whole area around you. As this expansive feeling continues you are no longer aware of distance and all becomes One.

What more can we say about Oneness? It is the truth about your spirit. Your spirit and the Great Spirit are One, for it is in you and in everybody and everything else, and so there can only be One.

When one goes deeper into the subject and even accepts Oneness as truth, the next step is *being* it and that is the hardest of all. The common thought is that you cannot be individual if you are the One but, in fact, it is the mind that keeps one separate, for in attempting to still the mind you are consciously acting to keep thoughts at bay. However, when you are fully absorbed in whatever is happening to you then you cannot be aware of any previous thoughts of individuality.

So, being at One, believing it and living it are different. Once it has been accepted that all is One the mind can come in and, the experience of Oneness disappears. It really is a matter of experiencing its fullness and then there is no need to talk about it or think about it. It just *is*.

It is good for your souls when you discuss philosophical matters at a deep level for it encompasses the fact that we are all One. You are correct to ask, to whom does one pray and whom does one thank if we are all One? Of course, you can still thank the One, for it benefits you to be grateful for your life and for everything that happens in it.

Until you completely understand and *know* that all is One and to experience it on a regular basis, then it is right for you to continue giving thanks. Even when you experience life as One you can still thank the One, the multiple as One, for your life and all it contains. Who else is there to thank? This is a very deep topic and not often debated.

When your thinking is along these lines you will no longer wish to judge because all is in you as you are in all. A person who is, in your terms, acting badly is still part of you and the one who is giving service in a loving way is also part of you. Continue with the thought that all is One and, in time, you will live that way. You will instinctively know that whomever you meet is part of you and you are part of them and, as your belief develops and becomes part of you, this will reflect on others you meet in a way they are not used to.

Remember, demonstrate by your manner, by your love, by your thoughts for others, that all life, all animals, all plants *are* One.

The enormity that the word 'Oneness' represents does not reveal its true meaning, for speaking the word without experience does not have the same effect. How can Oneness mean everything in both the physical and spiritual worlds? In fact, all are interconnected and, therefore, all is One. When you sit in meditation and think of Oneness how far does your mind extend? It doesn't need to extend at all because everything is within the One and the One is within everything.

You only have to think of Oneness; think of it within you and you will very soon be at One with all life. People use many things, many words, many thoughts, to assist them in meditation and being at One but, in fact, no words are necessary. Just being, that one word 'being', is all that is necessary but, again, the word means different things to different people so it is often better to think of being at One. This then gives the mind the thought that there is only One.

This is difficult to appreciate as you are living in a physical body and encounter many diverse people. You see the news; you read the papers and you often witness arguments, whether on TV or between people, and you see that at the time of argument those concerned are only thinking as an individual. If they thought only of the One there would be no argument, for who would they argue with? Oneself! So, it is all rather pointless and useless.

We know everyone has been in situations where they become a little agitated for very good reasons and it is then easy to forget who you really are. However, as your understanding grows and as your experience of Oneness increases you will not want to get involved in arguments. You will not want to judge, although we realise that is very difficult for you on earth. Nevertheless, if you keep the thought of Oneness with you at all times when about to make a judgement, you will be aware that you are only judging yourself.

As one experiences Oneness, the beauty, the bliss, when all around you seems to be *you*, then your life becomes more natural: you do not have so many confrontations. You will still be put into situations where in the past you may have become agitated but now something within makes you refrain from getting too involved. This is because the effects of Oneness on the individual are such that you no longer feel the need to argue.

Once you have experienced the wonderful feeling of being at One you begin to live it, realising that in your day-to-day life you and everyone you meet are the same. You are interconnected and, therefore, you are in them and they are in you, just as God is in you and you are in God. To think of Oneness means happiness, for your real self is always at One, and when mind, body and spirit are in harmony you will have a sense of satisfaction, peace and equilibrium.

It is easy to talk about Oneness; it is easy to say one has experienced Oneness, but to feel Oneness continually whilst on earth is another matter. Most people who are following their spiritual pathway have experienced Oneness in short spells, when everything stands still, when one feels enveloped by love, when one feels the whole world within, where there is silence and, yet, the silence is booming. It is difficult for people to continue in Oneness, but that is the aim of those who have experienced it. Once you are open, and connected to your God and all of spirit, then that is what you really are, the One Spirit; you are One with all.

In your quiet moments, when you feel that Oneness, how do you take it into your daily lives when you are with people, when you are listening to someone or when you are working in some way? If you become totally absorbed in what you are doing then you are at One, but when relaxing or thinking about something it is then that most people forget about Oneness.

Oneness is within all people all the time, but the secret is being aware of that Oneness every moment. However, we have said that when you are lost in what you are doing you are at One, which appears contradictory. It isn't really, it just means that for a time you had let go. Letting go of the physical, letting go of the ego leads into Oneness. So, try and place in the background of your life the awareness of Oneness and it *will* be there. It is always there, but the secret is knowing it is there and experiencing it.

Some people have many moments of Oneness, short periods and longer periods, but most have yet to permanently experience Oneness. We encourage you to let go, let go and let God run your lives. You will not be giving everything up, you will be receiving everything! You have the Totality of life when you are at One and could do anything. It is having the confidence that you are at One, knowing that God is in you and you are in God.

We refer to the Oneness that we all crave to experience. We know it is beyond description and when in that state there are no busy thoughts and worries in the background. We are in touch with our very self, the very centre of our being which is, of course, the Great Spirit. The spirit is all around, above, below, and within. It is in all things, even discarnate objects.

Why are you not in a state of Oneness more often? Why isn't it your natural state in the physical? Good questions. The main answer, and one of the reasons for incarnation on earth, is to find your real self, and to become One with it and with all life. The other major reason is to find love and be that love; be and experience unconditional love. In fact, the two go together. If you have one, if you are giving out unconditional love and your whole effort and concentration is in that experience, then you are at One. Think back to when you have helped others, and in the act of helping nothing else is in your mind. You are just being and doing; the doing is a result of being, and love and Oneness is that being.

How do you spend more time at One? The traditional way is to be in meditation and to gradually centre yourself and lose all connection with outside life. You can also be at One when you are living your normal day-to-day lives with thoughts of the One, whether working, thinking, or relaxing. When you are aware that all around you, and within you, is silent and peaceful you are at One. When you are entirely engrossed you are at One, without even realising it.

So, you can develop this Oneness even if you have no time for meditation. It can become a habit and is, again, similar to love in action; you could call it Oneness in action. You would not think it possible to be at One when there is movement, but when the mind is totally absorbed you are living in the moment and at One.

Striving to be in the moment enables one to be in touch with the inner soul, the inner spirit, where there is peace beyond understanding. Here one can touch the purity of love, All That Is. Have you any idea what that means? When you speak of spirit you generally mean those living on our side of life. You also refer to the spirit within you, and you refer to the Great Spirit as 'all there is'. So, what can be the essence of spirit?

The essence is like the nucleus of the atom. It is the inexplicable intelligence of all life; it is the spark of light, it is the Big Bang of physical life. It is the unknown, unfelt, beauty, and when you are able to touch that then you are in the centre of God. Can you imagine that? You have been at One at times and you have felt overcome with bliss, overcome with purity of thought, overcome with joy, with happiness, but you can go beyond that to the essence we speak of, for there is always something further to learn, something further to experience in life.

You may have had many wonderful experiences, but until you touch the essence you will have no idea what is behind all life. So, how can you reach that essence? We say to you go within, stay within, and during your day make time to consciously sense that you are at One with all. This will become a habit; it will form the pattern of your life and you will not do anything without being aware that you are in touch with reality. When you have done this for a while you will feel at One most of the time.

If you can imagine being at One throughout your day, that will lead on to not only experiencing but *being* the essence of life.

Do you ever wonder what Oneness means, what the connection is through every living being on the earth, every being in all the universes and every being in spirit on our side of life? How could anyone possibly imagine what that is like? You only have a very small sense of it when you are happy, when you are feeling open to all life, and sometimes in meditation.

We help you in those situations for we are able to feel that Oneness too. People think that when they transfer to our side of life everything is perfect. In one way it is, but there is still so much learning to do. One doesn't change character immediately and goes through a time of retrospection on the life just lived, wondering why one did this or that, but at the same time also being pleased with achievements.

All is One, but it takes time for anyone, wherever they are, to really appreciate what it means. We, in spirit, may be more aware than you but neither do we have full understanding. We have yet to feel continually at One or, should we say, *knowing* that we are.

We have much to do on our side of life, especially at this time with many souls leaving the earth unexpectedly. We have a two-pronged job. On the one hand we are helping those who come to us in great need, and at the same time helping people who try to bring heaven closer to earth. All is working as it should be, for the great plan of our Father God is perfect. He knows everything. He knows what will happen in a minute, He knows what will happen in a hundred years, He knows what will happen in a thousand years' time and in many millennia. So, you can be relaxed and leave everything in your life to the Great Spirit, knowing that all will turn out as it should, with no need for concern.

People worry for many reasons. There are those who dislike upsetting others, some who fear being badly thought of. Again, this is ego. What is the ego, or little self? Is it something solid, or in the mind? It is, of course, a figment of the imagination which appears to grow when someone is very self-centred, but everyone is born with the instinct to look after oneself and one's family. When you live by the heart there is no need to consider the ego for it has retreated to the background, where it should be, but can very easily come out of the box again.

Nevertheless, by helping others and living from the heart instead of the head, the ego will gradually lose its dominance.

Relax! Everything is perfect in God's kingdom within. It is in the reflection where confusion can arise, reflection being the material world. When looking in a mirror the reflection is only an image and not reality. Remember, when hardships and difficulties arise in life, that it is all a reflection, an illusion, for reality is the spirit within.

Scientific discoveries show that nothing in the physical world is actually solid although, of course, it appears so. Just as there is space between the planets and stars there is space within every atom and, consequently, all physical manifestations contain space. How does this affect the way one lives life on the earth plane?

You are not expected to walk through walls and break open logs with bare hands, but realising that everything in the material world is not as it appears can lead one to enquire beyond the physical. You are spirit with a body, not the other way around, and deeper spiritual investigation reveals the body to be impregnated with spirit, God's Spirit which is in every atom. Scientists have suggested there is a link or connection between atoms, again giving credence to the ancient wisdom of advaita, nonduality, meaning that all is One.

To bring nonduality into one's own life means removing the little I, me, the ego. Putting this into practice during meditation can produce remarkable results, for the deeper one goes the more one loses the ego. Expansion takes place within and, gradually, a feeling of Oneness permeates the whole being as the reality of connection with all life takes place, and mind barriers and limits are removed.

As you continue to go deeper within, having left behind all thoughts and attachments to the body, you are in a state of euphoria. You feel, and are, connected to everything near and far as you experience nonduality, or Oneness with all life, both physical and spiritual.

As you open up within, what do you experience? What do you see? What do you feel? What do you hear? Is everything so silent that you can hear a pin drop? You may sense something within which is warm, and a movement in your heart area. You may be aware of being in a sacred place, for in the middle of your spiritual heart is the Great Spirit who links through all life, through all individuals, as One.

As you feel love in the heart centre you may see a golden colour, you may see an amazing bright light and you will be enclosed by what can only be described as unconditional love. Everything before you, behind you, above you, below you, and in you, creates a blissful feeling. There is nowhere that love is not, for love *is* the Great Spirit. The Great Spirit is within you, so His love is also within you, and as you begin to understand there is no real separation in life you will feel an expansion of this love.

First of all, it increases within your body right to its extremities. It is all around you and is growing, growing and growing until the whole room feels blissful. Being in an earthly body one tends to think of physical limits, but by going beyond the body you are removing those limits. Your senses are aware of this great love expanding further and further out until the whole of your perception of distance is covered by that love, because you have no idea of the enormity of the universe and you cannot comprehend the scope of this Oneness of which you are a part.

The love continues to increase and it will never stop except when your mind comes in and again puts limitations on your life. In the meantime, feel the expansion, feel the wonder of Oneness as long as and as far as you can. Your spiritual self, the ultimate Spirit within, can take you anywhere you desire and, although this is not necessary, you know within that your life has opened up and gone beyond anything you have previously experienced. The Oneness all around you, within you, and beyond you, is always there.

The effect it has, when you are aware, is difficult to explain in words but it is, it just *is* and you will take this feeling as a memory as you proceed with your life. Once experienced in this way you will never forget and it will enhance your physical life, for you have that proof of being at One, having that feeling of being the nucleus of all life, for the God who is in you and all life, is indescribable and beyond any thought. Nevertheless, that is who you really are and when you have opened yourself completely then you *are* the living God.

These words are offered to you in friendship and in love of the Great Spirit, for we are all One if you could only realise it at all times. You hear these words and sometimes feel a connection with another person, occasionally a connection with spirit and, very rarely, you can experience a connection with all life. How does this happen?

It cannot be achieved, for it already *is*. It is just a matter of letting go of thoughts, prejudices, conditioning, anything that distracts from a pure open mind. It is not a matter of thinking of Oneness, although this can help but, rather, forgetting all attachments.

In going beyond the normal limits of the bodily mind one transcends all thoughts and is at peace. This results in the whole self being lifted into another dimension, but with the physical body remaining in the same position. The real self, the spiritual self, gives the feeling of being lifted, of being other-worldly, into the wonderful state of Oneness. You will seem to be in and part of a vast, peaceful and loving place where you are at the centre of everything, both physically and spiritually.

You are now experiencing Oneness when all time is forgotten, for your real self, your spirit, is timeless. There is no need for thoughts or words for these inhibit the experience. Your inner being now seems to expand beyond any limits you had previously placed on yourself, consciously or unconsciously.

Without realising it, you are at One with your spirit and the One Spirit of all life.

Chapter Ten

Realising Spirit Within

Life is a dream. You have all experienced exciting dreams, full of action and full of friends, those who have passed and those who are on your earth plane. When you have a memorable dream it is, at the time, as though it were happening in your reality. So, too, is the dream you are living today, the only difference being that you are not aware this life is a dream. Why is this, and how can one benefit from the understanding?

Your life is a dream because it is not the reality of spirit; it is a reflection of the subconscious mind. The only reality is the Great Spirit, which activates and allows what appears to be your life in the *apparent* human body. We know that it feels like your only life but when you are able to forget, to go beyond the body and become at One in the fullness of the Great Spirit, you will be aware only of the one Reality.

You may think this is all very well, but reason that whilst in the body you still need to live your earthly lives. This is quite right; so true. We would respond by saying it is in God's plan that you believe your earthly life to be a reality until you gain the understanding that there is more to life than the apparent one you are living.

This subject is not one you can discuss freely, for most people are fully occupied living their life with all its attendant excitement, problems and diversions. However, all who realise that there is no death, and especially those with experience of the next life, Oneness, and a knowing that one is not the body, are ready to absorb the knowledge that life on earth is but a dream.

Lift up your hands in joy and praise to the Great Spirit. You, who have experienced within the peace, the silence of the Spirit, know that He is within all life. You realise that you are consciousness, that the body is within and intermingled with spirit. There is no death and, therefore, your lives can be an offering to the Great Spirit, a service to Him and all mankind.

You accept communication with us, which can be like talking to one another on earth. This is when you are an open channel with love in your heart and an expectancy for joining together the two worlds. When you are in this state of mind, when your heart and mind are open, then you will not be disappointed as we have much to convey to you which will be used in the days ahead as you transmit this knowledge to your fellow man.

We come to you on a high vibration where we can meet in love and joy to proclaim the glories of heaven and the Creator. As you sit with open hearts we become as One, overcoming the barriers of the two worlds. You will feel a quickening of the heart, and as love pours in and fills every cell so your vibrations fill our hearts. As we become one there is an exchange between the two worlds with knowledge and wisdom filling your aura together with colours, the beautiful rays from spirit. As you maintain this connection so the combined colours of love and healing are sent out into your world and, gradually, as more and more people do likewise so the energies will fall on those in need and will reach the very hearts of people.

So, continue to look up, look within, open your hearts to All That Is, and you will be filled with the grace of the Great Spirit.

The word 'consciousness' brings forth many thoughts and different meanings for people as they ponder what this word, that really describes life above the normal conscious state, actually means for each individual.

It infers some vastness beyond the human mind, an intangible macrocosm wherein all life, both human and spiritual, exists. It is the Oneness, a universal soul, through which the Great Spirit's silver thread activates and maintains this glorious heaven.

It is the state reached in meditation when all physical thoughts and actions are stilled, leaving and opening a vista of riches beyond the normal mind's experience. As one floats in this sacred river of love, feelings of bliss and manifold pleasures are felt when one is immersed in this treasure of spirit.

Consciousness contains the whole spectrum and foundation of existence and is like a parallel spiritual universe where the essence of all life resides. No matter whether you have a physical body or live in the spiritual realms, you are part of this one all-containing lake of Godliness.

It is your inherent being and *is* you, is *in* you and *you* are in It. You are intrinsically part of It but can also be aware of your primeval base within its glorious ever pulsating and ever-changing magnificence.

The world around you is filled with love, the love of the Creator. The air itself is full of love; it gives life and, although you cannot see it, it is filled with the most glorious array of light. Although you are accustomed to seeing the rainbow, this is like a thousand rainbows. As you breathe this wonderful life force so the colours and energy fill your whole self, radiating and illuminating it; you are like little stars in the darkness. Many souls enjoy the experience of being on earth and all have a role to play in the *one great purpose* of life, but some wander around in an aimless state.

We see you helping one another; some more than others. We see the light brighter in some and, when we come closer, we notice that when your spiritual hearts are open you reach further than the physical, for the love within propels you ever forward into the arms of the Great Spirit. All have within them a yearning to return to the Great White Spirit. As your being awakens to the glories of nature, of the spirit within all life, you will see the connection of Oneness between you all and everything and everyone around you. When your spiritual eyes are open you will see this connection as a beautiful picture and you can trace the light coming to you, surrounding, going within you all, and continuing its journey between all life.

As you move with more understanding so you will feel uplifted, both mentally and physically, and you will be ready to experience the inner life of light, truth, peace, wisdom and the purest love.

'I have been watching your circle progress; I have been watching particularly the love and healing that you exude instinctively. To be able to do it automatically takes something rather special, and it is not earned just from one lifetime, but you have all experienced so much in your lives.

'I go further: you actually share it with many on our side of life for, as usual, there is a host of spirit friends with you this morning. They have come to witness what happens in your circle. Most of them have never experienced anything like it, either when they were on the earth or now that they are in spirit. So, we welcome them as we welcome you.

'You have the understanding that there is much more to life than can be seen in front of you. You know that you are more than what you seem to be. You know that all around you the grasses, the trees, the beautiful flowers, the animals, all life in the sea and on land, contain such beauty. The beauty we are talking about is within nature, as it is within you. If you imagine the brightest light that you have ever seen, and multiply it several thousand times, you would get some idea of the light, the power, that is within all life on earth.

'Each time you look at a person, or an animal, imagine what is beyond the physical and we, on our side of life, will help you to open your minds to the wonder of the invisible life. You know that the physical objects you see are not what they seem. They have so much space within them, within their atoms, within their make-up, that you would marvel at how they are kept together. You know, of course, that it is by the grace of God and, also, that your bodies work as they do for the same reason. All life on earth is because of the One Life, the one great intelligence.

'How can you see more of the invisible? Not just those in spirit but everything that is before you, including your own bodies, the chairs you sit in, the ground you stand on and the heavens above you. Open your minds and ask for help to see the reality of what is and you will be amazed. You may have seen colours associated with people and objects but go far deeper and see the *real* spirit.

'Nobody "sees" the Great Spirit. They are sometimes aware of Him and sense Him within and around them but when you see the reality within you, and within all life, you will be aghast. You will want to stay in that state, and retain that vision always. Reality is around all of you, within all of you; I see it in the air, and the air has such beauty. Spend a little time and ask for help so that you may have the gift of truly seeing.

'I have enjoyed spending time with you today and I encourage you to go forward in your lives, to go forward and spread your love wherever you go.'

You raise your hearts and minds to us and we are able to communicate with you, for we pick up your love.

As the Great One has said, as you change yourself, you change your neighbourhood, the town changes, the country changes, and the world will change. What does this mean and, even more importantly, what does this entail? It means accepting that you are more than the physical body. We know you are aware of it but do you always show it? Are you always aware of what is beyond the physical? Are you aware it is a dream you are living?

When you go beyond the dream you are then into the reality of life, for the reality of life is your true self, is the true self of everyone around you, of all life, of the earth itself, for what do you think keeps the earth giving forth its bounty? It is, of course, the Great Spirit within the earth, for the Spirit is within all.

Once you are aware of this, it allows you to look at your life and people around you in a different way. It allows you to look forward with confidence in all that you are doing; it allows you to think of others in a positive way. You don't even need to think of their physical bodies or their names; you just think of their spirit. As you do so you are sending out healing, and increasing the vibrations around you.

You begin to change, to spend more time aware of the spiritual, to have that loving feeling within when you are doing anything, especially when you are working and thinking of others. As you progress in this life, so your soul is progressing throughout each life and builds up such growth, love, and light which is within you now and will be for all time, whatever body you may occupy.

Think about who you really are; think about who others really are. When you come across someone who is not exactly giving you love then remember who they really are and they will receive love through their spiritual bodies. This is how your world will change. Think of the downtrodden areas of your cities: remember that everything within those cities, everybody and everything, is spirit. Think of them as spirit and that will transform them.

It may sound too good to be true, too easy, but when you are busy, when you are engrossed in something then you are engrossed in the Spirit. So, just take this forward in everything you do, in everything you think, to everyone you meet.

You do not let misadventure affect your beliefs because with you it is a *knowing* that the Lord resides in you. How could it be any different? Have you ever wondered how your bodies move, think, and live? It is amazing that you are all so different in looks, in mannerisms, and beliefs.

It can only be because the Great Spirit is within you all. Doctors think that once the heart starts the body will continue to live but, in reality, unless the spirit is within the life form then that life cannot live, cannot exist. Therefore, the spirit comes before the heart starts to beat. Conversely, when the spirit is ready to leave the body, the physical body begins to close down as preparations are made for the individual soul, which contains the spirit, to move to the next life.

It is good that you are aware of the spirit within you, that *is* your life, for it is a two-way experience. The Great Spirit created life so that He could live through you, live through everyone and experience in so many different ways. You, in turn, live through the Great Spirit and, when you are open to the glorious wonder that He is, then your lives will take on a different meaning. You will have more awareness; your love is turned into actions of kindness, of healing, of little things which mean so much in people's lives.

If you can be aware of the Great Spirit experiencing with you then you can let your *self* go and let Him live through you, the ultimate being the dual experience of God and yourself. Added to that, the thought of Oneness accentuates your living for you can then feel at one with the person you are speaking to, with any animal that may be present, or, indeed, with all life.

Be at peace, in the knowledge that the experience you think is yours alone is that of the Great Spirit also and the Great Spirit's experience is yours. What a wonderful revelation!

What are you looking to achieve? What are you here for? What are you expecting? It would be futile for you to try to answer these questions. Who does the achieving and who receives the rewards?

When you realise that all is One, when you realise that you *are* spirit, that you have within you the Great Spirit, then how can you claim that you, individually, own anything, achieve anything, even want anything? Your real self has everything it needs. It is your outer shell, your lower self, that thinks it is here to gain, to look for riches; whereas, as we have said already, your real self has everything that you need.

With this understanding where does it place any of you, individually, with the knowledge that you are all connected; by you we mean your higher and lower self. You *have* both and you *are* both. Sometimes greed and other sensory desires lead you into the backwaters of life, or into new experiences, depending upon which way you look at it. You are here on the earth to experience life, to experience friendship, love. You are here to serve, you are here to realise that you are love, you are here to realise that you are yourself God.

Most people would think that statement very wrong. How can you be God? You are God, everybody is, they just don't realise it. It is useless proclaiming this for you will be given short-change by most people you meet. However, to enjoy and experience life on earth it is important that you are aware and understand this truth, for you are then better able to handle the problems that you meet. When you know you are here for a purpose then you can go along with what life gives you. So, does it matter if you go down dark alleyways? No, not really but, of course, you take the consequences.

We have asked the question, why do you really think you are here? There are many books, there are many teachers that will explain reincarnation. They will explain that you cannot learn all you need to learn in one lifetime. Whilst this is correct, the real reason you are here is to find and be the love of the Great Spirit. When you become One with all life you are that love, you give out such beautiful thoughts and rays that cannot be seen but can be felt by your fellow men and women.

When you have found that love, and when you are that love, your life is so fulfilled because that love is within you. You do not plan what to do, it just happens. You do not have to think, for the more you think it stops the flow. When you know you are love you will have a wonderful effect upon those around you, and all thoughts of previous lives go out of the window; you are living in the moment. You do not wish to think about the past or the future as you have an amazing feeling within. You are timeless, you have everything you need: you do not need riches, you do not need material things other than a bed and simple food.

However, by being at One, you will have an amazing life; every breath of air will seem so precious to you. Every movement within your body, even if you are unable to move as freely as you once did, will not affect your equilibrium. You will have complete love and may be unable to express how you feel, but by your expressions, your actions, and your words, others will know and realise you have found the secret of life.

When you completely lose yourself, when you open to All That Is, you feel as though you are in-between worlds in a special place of your own. You could call it heaven, for it is peaceful, loving and endless; you can travel anywhere in it and from it. Once you have found this place you know it is special and, as such, we can work with you as your channels are open.

As you go through life, remember to go into your special place and we will always meet you there. It can be a quiet space where you can recharge your batteries and rejuvenate yourself and it can also be the most glorious connection with your God.

When you are ready and we are ready we can talk through you, but the primary reason for you to be in this space is for your whole being to experience the love of the Father. Once you are there the feeling will grow and, eventually, become Oneness. There is no need for thoughts, words or deeds: it is a place where you just *are*. You are in the I AM.

Rest awhile and bathe in the beauty of the moment.

'All That Is'; what a wonderful expression! You have some idea of what is meant by it and, at the very least, it means everything that is around you. It is the spirit within and around you; it *is* the Totality, and with Totality you literally have everything at your fingertips.

You talk about being at One with All That Is and that does, indeed, mean being at One with everything and everyone, including being at One with the spirit within. In essence all are the same, but an individual can appear to be different due to the *personality* projected to others.

If life were simple, just like turning on a tap, things would not be the same. There would not be the challenges you all need and there would be nothing to aim for. Neither would there be bliss or the special feelings experienced when the Great Spirit is known to be with you.

If it were as easy as turning a tap the supply would be automatic as it is with the flowers and trees who bring sap up into their leaves and branches during spring and summer. They know what time of year it is, they know when to shed their leaves and they know when to create buds. However, as humans, you are the blessed ones for you make your own decisions.

You decide the time when you wish to explore within, when you want to explore the spirit, when you realise there is more to the body than the physical. As you search within you eventually come into the very nucleus of Spirit. You come into the nucleus of peace, the heart centre of love: the stillness beyond thought. When in that stillness everything appears to stop, for you are in the moment; you are then open to the whole universe and you are completely open to the Great Spirit.

The moment is the time when you leave all your cares and problems behind, so make the most of it and stay as long as you can. It will greatly benefit your spiritual growth and your physical well-being.

You have that feeling within of nonduality as you become at One with your real self, with All That Is. Nonduality is a deep, deep, subject and one that is more about experience, or non-experience. It is about losing the individual self, letting it go into the background so that the real self takes over, entering that timeless zone where thoughts, worries, problems all disappear. They dissolve into the mass of thoughts that are all around, that are in the atmosphere, that are close to you, and are easily absorbed when one is chasing material aims and goals.

The opposite is true when at One with the spiritual aspect of one's being. There is no need for words when one is in a state of bliss, in the garden of Eden: in your heaven in and beyond your horizon, where the sun pours down its great light and energy, where the heat is in the background for this is the spiritual sun.

In this state, where everyday thoughts and feelings disappear into the background, the spiritual comes to the fore and you, the real you that is connected to all life, *are* the God Spirit within. This is nonduality. You feel Oneness all around you and, as you stay in this moment of Oneness, you are All That Is. You feel you are the centre of all life, the centre of the universe, the nucleus of the atom, the very centre of your being where the Spirit is located.

Rest awhile, take in the energy, the love, the peace beyond understanding. Take in the Totality for you are that Totality, you and all who are connected to you, at this frozen moment in time.

When you re-enter your physical world, you will be recharged. Every cell in your body will feel alive and all your muscles will be ready for the race, the race of life, with the Great Spirit at the centre, the goal of life.

You know you are all on a journey back to the Great Spirit, that indescribable, intelligent, magnificence that is our God. Talking about Him, Her, or however you wish to describe the One and Only Life, brings to mind His love that, again, is indescribable. It has such a far-reaching effect, for it covers the physical and spiritual universes as a beautiful blanket that is non-physical, and yet can be sensed. It envelops everyone and everything in its path and you only have to touch the very edge of it to receive the fullness of His love. At this moment you are enfolded by His love. It has a warm feeling, it has an inspired feeling, a wanting to reach out and be at One with it.

As you are absorbed in this love, you can get some idea of life when one rejoins the Great Spirit. There are very few who have totally merged with Him and even they still come back and help mankind. When you reach the end of the path it is just a little bit like the feeling in this room at the moment. It is, as we have described before, the Oneness of all life. You may wonder why, when you have touched on this Oneness, you cannot be in it forever. Well, you can, but it is not that easy, especially for you on the earth. Your minds come in and you think about what has to be done and, in fairness to you, you do have to provide for each other, you do have jobs to do and you do, at the moment, need to eat to survive.

All of this can, of course, detract from the goal of Oneness. Nevertheless, when you have, or make, the opportunity to sit and be at One with your Creator you will get some idea of what merging with Him would be like. This is a long pathway for most people, but when you have tasted this Oneness you will want it more and more.

We cannot describe heaven to you for it is not a place. It is a state of beingness within and if you have touched on it you can imagine what it is really like when experienced constantly. On our side of life, where we do not have physical bodies to hamper us, we have the advantage of being able to move, think and *be* very easily. As we progress we shed certain of our bodies and each one becomes lighter as we move on to the next stage. Ultimately, there will be 'no body' and we are not just talking about the physical, we are talking about the spiritual as well.

When there is 'no body' there, when you are no longer aware of a body, when you have gone beyond your personality, your character, then you are very close to the Creator. You can touch on it from time to time and what we advise you to do is to remember this wonderful feeling of Oneness. Take it through your lives so that you have it in your armoury, so to speak, as you go about your daily tasks, your happy times and your not-so-happy times. If there is no body present, then nothing really matters. Those words sound ridiculous to most people, but the true meaning, that you have been close to at times, gives you such an advantage for you know there is so much more to life than there appears.

As you progress through this life, remember you can only go through one life at a time and, as there is no time here, you can make the one life you have at the moment be your overriding life. When the time comes to drop off your physical body you will then just continue with that one life over here.

The secret of life is within, where the essence of light is to be found. Without this light, the very essence of the Great Spirit, physical life as you know it would not exist.

The secret is within every cell of your body and in all cells of all physical life on earth. You cannot see it, you cannot hear it, but you can be aware of it deep within the silence of the moment. *There* is the secret, the very powerhouse of your being. Becoming aware of it and feeling it simply means opening up the layers within until at the very heart, at the very centre of your being is the Great Spirit, this magnificence, this beauty, the Source of love, light and power.

Connect with it, bury your soul in it, surrender your personality to this love and it will embrace you and enfold you within its arms and transform you into a being of love and light. You will feel this love-energy within your veins as it reaches the very edges of your body, filling your whole being.

Relax into this Oneness and you will feel a connection with all life, not only as you sit in silence and contemplation, but also throughout your life when you have taken on board the Director and Founder of all life. Remain awhile, absorb love, light and peace in the silence and return to your essence, your infinite Spirit, as often as you can by just remembering who you really are.

There is within everything the innate beauty and substance of the Great Spirit which is connected to all people and beings, not only on the earth and in the heavens but throughout the universe, for where you see the physical there is also the spiritual counterpart. Whilst your individual lives can be compared to the microcosm, the entire dwelling place of God is the macrocosm.

What does this mean? It means that you are never alone, but also limitless. When you appreciate this, and are bold enough, then you can go beyond your limited frontiers. Even though you may be restricted in your physical bodies you are not restricted in the spiritual sense and, by connecting through your inner self to All That Is, you can be anywhere your soul directs.

Moreover, and more importantly, you can open yourself to the vast knowledge and wisdom that is awaiting exploration. When the soul is ready you can search from within the archives of time. The quotation, 'when the student is ready the teacher appears' applies to this internal enquiry. The first spiritual manuscripts ever written are available, as is God's eternal intelligence and this limitless sea of knowledge is available to all but will take time to reach. However, as you become adept at meditation, removing desires and seeking the One Great Spirit the vista of learning gradually opens.

You will know when you are receiving the pure white fountains of knowledge. Gradually, at first, you will be inspired and, as you bring into your life the closeness and awareness of spirit, you will open the doors to the university of all wisdom. When you reach this state, you will have permanently at your fingertips all that you require to be a teacher and master of your own destiny, but also the destiny of others who place themselves within your love and direction. You can then help them until they are ready to reach the mantle of Oneness themselves.

'You are in that space where anything can and will happen; just let go of your thoughts and let Me through.

'You think *you* have done this; you still cling on to things, cling on to your bodily pleasures, hurts and the sense of being individual. When you let go of the ego, or little me, you will run on air, ease through your life, feel as light as a feather and as smooth as a precision instrument.

'You are then ready for My work. You will have a direct line to Me and I will guide you through a maze of thoughts, take you to places and give you experiences you have never dreamed of. So, be at One with Me and, together, we will brighten the world and open doors within people which have been closed for too long.

'Relax and follow your heart. I shall always be there guiding you ever closer to your destination, to the fulfilment of your life's plan and reason for being here at this time. Remember, I AM love and where love is there is no fear.

'Relax now and await My presence.'

You reach Me in the deepest crevice of your heart. You don't have to perform days, months or years of spiritual practices to experience Me within, although this can be of help for some. It is more about thoughts, and the way you demonstrate your love for Me through your actions towards your brothers and sisters.

You are all on different pathways so don't judge one another but, rather, support each other and show real understanding. In making contact with your real self you will also be in touch with their real selves and, therefore, with Me.

Spend time looking inwards and you will become at One with Me and all life. You will at first notice a magnificent peace filling you and everything around you. You will want to touch the air in front of you, as it feels part of you. As you go deeper within, all sensation of time disappears and you will feel suspended in nothingness. A warm glow will fill your whole being and you will experience bliss beyond imagination. You are in the moment, in the *real* now, and all thoughts have long departed.

Allow yourself to stay in this moment for you are at One with Me. You can stay until your thoughts return, or you can move on to a deeper state of being ready to experience My heaven. Here, you will experience with Me pure love as a wonderful feeling for all life. You will be given a greater understanding of yourself, everyone, and everything in your life. You will have touched on the tiniest part of Me, but as All is One you can then be both the microcosm and macrocosm at the same time.

Having let go completely of your desires, petty thoughts and individualism, you will return to your physical state awakened to the Reality, and your future life will be governed by your internal connection with Me. The more you experience Me within the more you will feel and be aware of Me in your normal life. However, it will never be normal again as you will have an air of confidence and love surrounding you which will inspire you to give out words of comfort, understanding, wisdom and love.

You will never feel lost or bored again, for your life will be *love in action* as you follow your pathway with Me not just by your side but part of and at One with you.

It is a good morning wherever you are when you link in to your Father God, for when you go deep within you will find the Source of life, the Source of *all* life. You need not be in awe at that thought, that reality, for in truth you are spirit interpenetrated by your soul and body in this sojourn on earth. When you connect like this to your Creator your world expands, as you then have the ability to touch all life through the Spirit.

Notice the expansion within your body, the love of God which you can feel throughout your body and beyond, beyond the room, the house, your neighbourhood, as Oneness takes over your being. In this wonderful God-state you are able to send healing out into the world knowing that, through this Oneness, it will reach the furthermost parts of your world and all points in-between where there is a need.

As you continue to dwell in this Oneness of life your earthly thoughts have disappeared and been replaced by the One Thought. This thought is love, the love of the Creator, which is always in and around you and all life. It created physical life and continues to recreate in each moment of time on your earth. Dwelling in the Oneness, this nonduality recharges and inspires your physical bodies. From here all inventions take place in the minds of people, whether they have been sleeping or in a world of their own through music, art, or any activity which takes them beyond the conscious mind.

Being in the state of Oneness does not change one's personality immediately but expands its role in life as one becomes more fulfilled and open. Your whole being feels the Oneness of God as you take each new breath as though it was your first, for you will find your vision and experience of this life will take on a whole new meaning. You will have greater understanding of your fellow man and the animal kingdom as you take this feeling of Oneness into your daily life. You will feel an explosion of love not known before and compassion for all life.

So, although you will physically still be in the same body, you will have become a complete person and others will see it in you. Relax and enjoy this feeling as you have found the secret of life, with God beside and within you.

We join you at this beautiful time of day on your side of the earth before most people are awake and moving; when most things are still and when you can be in contact with your real self. What is your real self? It is that part within where you can go to experience the peace and love of the Father. It is the spirit within all beings, the spirit that is connected to all life. As you make your contact with God, your higher self, you feel uplifted. Your body is quiet as you reach upwards into the light. The light, of course, is within, but it is natural to seek it by looking skywards.

As you become still, the peace envelops you leaving you in a state of bliss. All worldly thoughts and conditions are left behind as you go deep within into the silence. You have now reached a point where the outside world is shut off and you are in the *now*, that second that seems to last forever, and you are only aware of the breath of your body. Peace extends beyond you, and it seems that you are in a bubble which is ever-expanding, taking in your house, your garden, your neighbourhood, the whole area around you. As this grows and grows beyond the area you are familiar with, so your whole being expands with peace and love.

Stay awhile in this heaven, for it is within you, and as you feel heaven all around it is spreading throughout your being. You can recognise it with a tingling, a satisfaction; Oneness with all life. You can stay like this for one second or for one hour: it is timeless to you, your spirit and the Great Spirit.

Something within will bring you back to the body, to your usual conscious self, but your timeless, blissful experience will stay with you throughout your day giving you the peace and assurance that all is well in your particular world. You will then project the love and light which has been within you. You will project it wherever you go and you will be aware of this wonderful experience as you go on your way and spend your day in the knowledge that the Great Spirit is with you always.

We are as One at this moment; we are as One always, but for you on the earth it is difficult to maintain that feeling, that knowledge of Oneness. You go through many experiences yet there are times, not only in meditation but also when fully engrossed, when you are overcome with love, as though the whole world is within you and you are the whole world.

As this feeling develops you *are* in the moment and life stands still; this moment seems as though it is lasting forever, for you are the Great Spirit, you are the Christ. In this moment you are everything and you feel something akin to bliss, more than peace. It is, of course, love expressing itself within you.

Why does that feeling not last forever? Simply because your minds come in, you think about what is happening and then you have lost the moment. There is no criticism in that for you are on the earth. What we would say is when it happens again remember to put all thoughts aside, for it is thought that induces separateness. Everyone is at One with all things, with all life: the only trouble is one doesn't immediately realise it. Until one does, one does not have the benefit, the wisdom, the understanding and, above all, the communication with the spirit within.

Spirit can be described in many ways, but it is of the Great Father. It is the strongest connection one can have and, by communicating with the Spirit, you will not only have a special feeling within but you will have all the knowledge you need for any given situation. The now, as we have said, can extend forever as it does with the Great Spirit. Therefore, you also have the opportunity to live in that state forever.

We know this is not practical one hundred percent of the time on earth but, if it was so, imagine what you could do. You would have all the power you need to help not only yourself but all those around you. You would know it could only be done by the will of God for, if you took that power and used it unwisely, the repercussions would be greater than the existing problems and they would rebound on you. So, a great responsibility accompanies the power that is inherent within you, but to get to that stage one has to first be regularly in touch with the Great Spirit.

As you experience this timeless zone, where there is no thought, your whole being will be filled with the light of heaven. As you continue in this timeless state you will be given all the reserves of light, energy, love, peace, and wisdom that you will need in the coming days.

So, change your thinking when you are going about your normal work, when you are talking to people, when you are relaxing. Remember who has given you this life; think of the One and your life will become a treasure. Each breath will feel like gold within you; it will make everything sparkle within. The energy levels, that are normally lower as one ages, will become much greater. You can always find time for a moment or two of communication within. Whatever you are doing you can enter that state for a brief moment and, once there, you will receive all the help you need.

Let go and let God. It sounds simple, doesn't it? It should be; but letting go, letting go of what?

Letting go of the mind, thoughts, fixed ideas, opinions, dogma, and letting in purity, the purity of Spirit. You will then think without preference, prejudices and experience. Imagine clear thinking, so pure it is like a silver arrow not deviating from its path. How beautiful is the pure Spirit that transforms the inner being of a person and thus the outer: heard in speech and seen in a smile, a caring look.

The purity of Spirit is like an angel walking before you, preparing the way, and taking you where you need to go. The purity of Spirit can be felt within the heart, enfolding you in love. As you experience that love let it expand to all parts of your body. Then, as your fingertips are tingling, as your heart centre is warm and expanding, love will go forth from you out, out, into the wide world, and while it continues on its way you are enfolded in deep peace.

You know the love is going forth and you can feel an expansion of the spiritual aspect of your being. Within your body each organ is opened up with energy from the Source of all life. Words are irrelevant to the feeling, the satisfaction, the connection with All That Is.

You feel alive, you feel ready to run a mile, to fly to the mountain tops, for your mind has also expanded leading you forward to new glories within. You then have a yearning to search for the centre of all life. You have reached it, but it appears that you are travelling at great speed where everything is whizzing past you. You are, in fact, unmoving in the centre.

You feel you could go further into nothingness. As you move, slowly at first, you realise you are back where you started, the only difference is that you now have awareness beyond description as everything around you pulsates with love. You have been on a journey within life, within each cell, within each atom, within the space of each atom and within the heart of God.

How do you keep on an even keel throughout your whole life? Until you have surrendered to All That Is you cannot. By surrender we don't mean giving up; rather, we mean the opposite, by taking on the mantle of the Great Spirit. People generally think that surrender is something of a backward step in life, but nothing could be further from the truth.

Surrender means going beyond the physical ups and downs of life into the Christ Spirit of tranquillity, of love, feeling yourself leapfrogging into a higher level of thought, thus rising above the daily trivialities and bodily desires of the senses which keep one close to earthly conditions.

Taking that leap of faith into the unknown is difficult whilst in a physical body and being a slave to the cause and effect of worldly life. In going beyond the physical, beyond the mind, one will go into the silence, the deeper silence that has to be experienced to be believed, a silence where earthly worries are left behind.

One will feel lifted up, metaphorically speaking, into a wonderful mode of love and light which can be felt pulsating within. At first this can be experienced in meditation but, as one gradually becomes more adept at reaching this higher level, it is possible to feel this state at all times, eventually becoming aware of its permanence in the background of one's whole being.

Instead of surrendering the ego, one will actually expand into the heavenly state of *being*: returning to the wonderful dimension of thought which was, in fact, the human quality when man first walked upon the earth.

'I have come to tell of realms unknown to you and, yet, within your grasp. These are the realms of spirit that can be attained through the inner being of the physical body. It sounds a contradiction, going inside to reach something which appears outside, but as everything and everywhere is connected to the Great Spirit then where better to make communication with these realms.

'So, sit and feel yourself going within, going further within, going to the very heart of your being. There you will find perfect peace, there you will find unconditional love, there you will find yourself being transported into our world. It will seem as though you are still going within when, in fact, you will be going direct to these Divine realms of spirit. As you link into us we show you the intricate drawings and patterns in the temples that are here. Oh yes, we have temples here as you do on earth.

'You sense the colour pink all around, which shows you there is such love here. The love, unconditional love, of the Father is all around as you feel lifted up, ever-upwards, into temple after temple. As you settle in, you will note that you are surrounded by angels, angels who are bowing to you and are ready to serve all who enter this sacred place. As the feeling of love becomes stronger you are on your knees in reverence to the Divine Spirit.

'You are taken into the next chamber where the walls are gold, but at the top there is an opening where you will pass through and be greeted by such a bright light that you have to shield your eyes. There in front are the Beings of Light. They are bringing you close to the centre of all life which is the brightest light you have ever encountered. You are given shields for your eyes as you sit in the presence of All That Is...

'You experienced a quickening of the heart which has now been stabilised by the incredible, perfect, peace. As you bathe in the beauty all around so you become at One with these surroundings and you feel you have truly found and realised the Spirit within.'

Who am I? This is a question that people have asked over eons. The Avatar Sai Baba has said that you are three people: the one you think you are, the one others think you are, and the one you really are. So, who is the one you really are?

Relax; sit still, go within, and now who do you think you are? Are you the body, are you the mind, soul, or are you spirit? You are told that you are spirit, droplets of the Divine. Are you droplets of the Divine, sons and daughters of God, or is every part, every cell and every atom of you Divine?

Again, you are told that Spirit, the Great Spirit, God, is within every atom of the universe and all living beings. If that is the case why don't most people realise it? It is probably because they have come to earth in a physical body to experience life in a material world.

It is only when you have had experiences beyond the physical world that you realise there is more to your being than the body. When you sit and meditate and go deeply within you have feelings of deep peace, pure love and bliss. It will feel, sometimes, as though you rise above the body and its attachments.

You are taught that there is only One and you are connected to all life. When you experience this, you have an inner knowing that it is the truth. You feel an expansion within that goes beyond the immediate vicinity and eventually becomes infinity.

It is impossible for me to describe the experience of Oneness, other than to say, 'I AM both everybody and everything, and everybody and everything is Me. This is the reality of who I AM. I AM All That Is and All That Is is Me.'

Live every moment as if it were your last and you will experience life as you have never before.

You will be awake to what is behind life, what is within a petal, what is within a tree, within a raindrop.

You will see beyond the physical, beyond the illusion, beyond the veil which has been in front of you all your life.

You will see the glory of Spirit as the vista opens up before you. You will be in the garden of Eden where all beings and colours will be beyond your experience and beyond your dreams.

You will have let go of the constraints of the body, of the mind, and your life, your vision will be multi-dimensional as you move forward with Me.

Each tiny step will lead you into the furthest depths of the unknown, where you will feel alive as your whole being expands, taking in and receiving beauty beyond and behind the physical.

I AM at One with all life. What a statement; what a huge meaning. Who is the I AM? What is the I AM?

To experience the I AM means to feel at One with the Great Spirit within every atom, every drop of rain, every single piece of grass, every molecule of air; *all* life.

As you go deeper within during meditation a stage is reached where, instead of feeling enclosed and smaller, you suddenly come into the vastness of the illumined space of infinity. A beautiful vista has opened up leaving you feeling part of, in fact being, the wholeness of creation.

Staying in this unfathomable greatness of Spirit you are no longer restricted by time and physicality. You are still aware of the physical body in the background, but as you are projected further into the beauty of nothingness it feels as though you are in the centre of the universe.

You are now in that space where the smallest dot and the largest planet is the same; for you are that dot, you are that planet. You are nothing and everything at the same moment, for there is only one moment and that is everlasting.

As the journey continues you see a magnitude of colours, bright and vivid, all intermingling with one another. As you travel further you feel weightless but still at the centre of life. You have now reached stillness beyond imagination, and you are at One with the very Source where the light is so bright you cannot look at it, but you *become* it. You are now in the centre of Oneness.

As you return slowly to the centre of your body you will feel invigorated and full of light, and you return to your material awareness having just experienced Oneness like never before.

When you are at One with your inner self you are at the centre of the universe, at the centre of all life. You can feel a pulse which is getting ever-stronger; it is the pulse of the Creator. It is heard in the body as the heart pumping, but it is also heard in the universe as supreme energy and that is what you are hearing now.

Stay in this vital energy; stay as close as *being*, being it, being the nucleus of all energy. You *are* the being, the cause of everything, as you sit at One with all life, as you sit at One with God.

As you continue to feel consciousness all around you, you are uplifted. It feels like light cascading outwards from you. You feel a warmth which is love itself. You feel the silence which is sometimes described as nothing, but even in nothing there is God. God is in everything, even in space and there is nowhere that God is not. There is nothing that does not contain the Great Spirit. You are in the Great Spirit; the Great Spirit is in you. The Great Spirit is you and you are the Great Spirit. Feel the consciousness surrounding you, enveloping you, being you and you being it, for you are at One with all life. You are experiencing the very centre of all life; it is like emptiness and, yet, emptiness is full, full of Spirit.

Your scientists keep searching for the origins of life; they seek in the physical world. They split the atom and are going deeper within the atom, but they have not found what you are experiencing at this moment. You have gone beyond the physical into the heart of God and from here you can be anywhere in the world or the universe that you choose to be. The only thing that holds you back is your own limitation, but as your self-made barriers are gradually removed you experience a little more of the truth of life.

Rest awhile in this great centre of life where the energy is permeating through not only the whole of your being, but everything around you. You are now experiencing the fullness of love, the fullness of the love of the Creator and, as you absorb this love, be ready to share it as you go through life.

Realising Spirit Within. What does this really mean? It means recognising and experiencing the Great Spirit within and knowing that all life is of Spirit. As one begins to feel happiness, peace and bliss within, one is on the road to full realisation of the truth of all life: Spirit, God, the Creator. That is all there really is! Call Him Love and the same applies; there *is* only Love.

The individual is the Great Spirit in disguise; as are animals, trees, flowers, the earth and the whole universe, for behind the physical or, rather, impregnated within the physical, is the power that connects all life. Thus, Oneness, when continually experienced is the living proof, the truth, that all are channels of the Divine.

To be at One with All That Is means realisation and complete freedom of the individual who has gone from the microcosm to the macrocosm.

Epilogue

From birth to death the earthly lifespan of a human being varies in duration: all lives are different, pre-determined and unknown to the individual. What opportunities! A life on earth with which to experience the feel of rain on the face, of sunshine on the body, the touch of a hand, a caress, the comfort of an arm around the shoulder, a kiss, falling in love, having children. All the time the soul within knows the past, knows the spirit, knows the journey, but the knowing is locked within one until investigation into the mystery of life and death begins.

Most people have no knowledge that life goes on after so-called death and are not aware of a previous life. This is because the greatest experiences can be achieved without prior knowledge of perpetual life. Everything occurs at the right time, and what a wonderful time, when one's being opens up into knowledge, belief and knowing. Previously, thoughts of what happens after death would normally be swept aside, but now there is an explosion of happiness, of searching for more knowledge knowing that when the time comes to leave the mortal coil a new expansion of life awaits.

How does this affect the individual? It takes away the biggest fear man has, that of death. It allows him or her to settle and, more importantly, to open up within: to be aware of the love of the Father, the love that tingles within every cell, the expansion in the heart area, the bliss extending throughout the body. What joy! What a breakthrough for the life that lies ahead, the knowing that life is infinite allowing one to be transformed into a spiritual being, aware of the real mind, body and spirit.

As the new pathway reveals itself, experiences within and without the body form the basis for the rest of one's life. Gradually, love of the Great Spirit will extend and become far-reaching; beyond imagination. The growing certainty of the Oneness of all life will become manifest, thus Realising Spirit Within.

Lightning Source UK Ltd.
Milton Keynes UK
UKHW041845311018
331548UK00001B/12/P